Shining in Infinity

Shining in Infinity
Charles McIntyre

atmosphere press

A Mirror in the Rain

We stand massed together in darkness,
Once safety but now danger resides in our numbers,
Once protection but now destruction lurks
in our campfires,
So we must remain mute and huddled together
for a lifespan
Our souls drenched by an eternal downpour of emotions,
Standing silently, shining in infinity,
All that we may ever be to each other are merely mirrors
in the rain.

John O'Bryan, Khe Sanh, March, 1968

CHAPTER ONE

The rain fell in gusty sheets along the lush green slope of Hill 881. Heavy monsoon clouds swirled around the hillside. Light could neither penetrate nor escape the heavy black night.

It had rained nearly every day for the past month in this mountainous northern corner of South Vietnam. Rain had first filled the mountain jungle streams. They were now raging torrents. The sound of rushing water floated on the wind like a chorus of whispers in the darkness.

The valleys flooded next, driving all forms of life to high ground.

The marines on Hill 881 occupied a prime piece of the high ground. Four months ago other marines had taken this 881-meter-high hill from a North Vietnamese battalion in a savage seesaw fight. The marines now had a circle of bunkers and gun emplacements about three meters from the top.

The deluge had eroded some of the dirt from the hillside. In one spot next to the marines' trash dump the soil washed away from a mass grave, exposing the bodies of the original North Vietnamese defenders.

The smell of death and wet rotting countryside blended, to form a particularly foul odor found only in places where civilization and nature have decayed. The marines were familiar with the smell but could never get used to it.

An Asian tiger stood sniffing the air at the bottom of the hill 881. He was starving, wet and tired. He smelled men, but did not know they were to be feared. He also smelled rotting flesh and knew there was food on the hill. Huge muscles bunched in the cat's shoulders as he cautiously moved upward. He was the hunter and the night belonged to him.

John O'Bryan sat at a listening post eighty-five meters from the top of the hill. He was also wet, tired and hungry. He lay on the soggy ground with a green poncho draped over him. The rain made it impossible to hear anything so he stared into a black void. During the monsoon season the war had come to a halt in the shifting mud. The weather prevented air strikes and reconnaissance missions. Nature enforced a ceasefire.

O'Bryan sat as he had been trained. He opened his eyes as wide as he could and moved his head slowly from side to side, in an attempt to pick up movement in the darkness. He tilted his head and slowly sat up. He thought he saw something move to his right front. If it was a North Vietnamese probe, he knew he would be safe for the moment.

He had made a great show of setting up his position behind a rock just before dark. As soon as darkness fell he crawled silently in the mud to his present vantage point. If he had been watched, his enemy would be looking for him behind the rock and he would be waiting with a hand grenade when they came for him. He smiled in the night. It was one of many little details you learned in combat, if you survived long enough.

O'Bryan sat watching the area surrounding the rock. The brilliance of a trip flare igniting to his right froze him in a blinding flash. Something enormous was moving quickly at him.

The great cat flashed by him at full speed. O'Bryan's

mouth sagged open as he watched the tiger run up the hill in the fading light of the flare. It amazed him that the cat seemed to moved in absolute silence. His senses gave him little confirmation of what he had seen. Only the lingering sulfur smell of the flare told him what he saw was real.

"L.P. Charley, this is Pine Pole Charley Actual, what have you got down there?" O'Bryan's hand shook as he reached for the radio handset clipped to his shirt pocket. His voice cracked in a semi-whisper. "Charley Actual I just saw the biggest damned cat of my life. He went past me headed uphill towards the perimeter."

"L.P. Charley say again?"

"A cat sir, a big tiger, he's probably inside the perimeter somewhere."

"OK L.P. Charley, keep alert, out."

Keep alert, O'Bryan thought. Like I'm going to take a nap out here after this. The skin on his legs prickled against the wet jungle pants. He had made far too much noise talking on the radio and the flare must have exposed his position. He considered moving again but decided against that. He knew the marines above him were now being put on one hundred percent watch and some sleepy eyed grunt might just throw a grenade if he spotted something moving down on the hillside. He tried to curl into a smaller ball under his poncho with the radio tucked under his legs.

Lt. Henderson, the platoon commander of third platoon Bravo Company, turned to Sgt. Alvarez. "Sergeant, inform all the men by landline that there is a tiger inside our perimeter. Pass the word to stand to one hundred percent watch. I want no shooting unless they have an identified target. If I hear shots there better be a dead cat out there."

"Yes, sir," snapped Alvarez. Alvarez walked to the other end of the command post bunker and picked up the battery-powered telephone. He cranked the small round wheel on the side, and the phones in each of the four squad bunkers responded with a metallic ring. He waited for each of the squad leaders to respond. He looked at his watch and noted that it was nearly 2 a.m. Finally, he had four groggy squad leaders on the phone.

"Good morning, people. We are now on one hundred percent watch. It seems there is a kitty cat inside our perimeter. This is a big, hungry kitty. So if you or your people don't want to end up as kitty crap, I suggest you stay in your positions and stay alert."

"Sarge, just how big is this kitty?" asked Corporal Johnson, the second squad leader.

"Johnson this kitty probably weighs about 600 pounds." There was a silence as each squad leader thought about it.

"Can we shoot at it Sarge?" someone asked

"The lieutenant says only if you got an identified target. He says if he hears shots, there better be a dead pussy out there. However if I was you people, I wouldn't do that. The only thing you're gonna do is piss that cat off if you shoot him with one of those little pea shooter M16s. Pass the word. See all you big game hunters in the morning." Sgt. Alvarez put the telephone receiver back in its cradle on the wall and smiled. He walked to his bunk made of wooden ammunition crates and sat down. He looked over at the young P.F.C. who sat on radio watch in the corner. "PFC Jordan, check with the listening posts every hour. Wake me up if anyone spots the tiger, or there is enemy contact."

"Ok sarge," replied Jordan who seemed to be deep in thought. "Sarge?"

"Yeah Jordan?"

"You think if I lit another candle it would help? I mean maybe the tiger wouldn't come in if the light was too bright?"

Alvarez smiled again as he lay back with his hands behind his head.

"Whatever you think Jordan, you're in charge of security in this bunker while me and the lieutenant are asleep. Just make sure the poncho is tight around the entrance, I don't want no gook sightin' a mortar round on our little C.P."

"Sure Sarge," said Jordan as he lit another white candle. He placed it on the wooden crate table next to him and felt much safer.

Back down the hill, O'Bryan was still wondering where the big cat had gone. He had once seen a dead water buffalo wedged in the crook of a tree limb twenty feet in the air. He had wondered who or what had put it there. To his amazement he learned that mountain tigers many times killed the local livestock and deposited them in trees for safekeeping. He gave a slight shudder under the poncho as he contemplated the strength required for such a task. A full grown Asian water buffalo weighed nearly a thousand pounds and was formidable in its own right.

He had kept his eyes squeezed shut now for ten minutes, trying to regain his night vision. Despite the cat's predatory skills, O'Bryan knew the deadliest thing roaming these mountains at night walked on two legs.

He opened his eyes again and scanned the darkness.

The shot of adrenaline he had received when the cat came by had almost worn off. He could neither fight nor run. Consequently the muscles in his legs twitched involuntarily.

He had momentarily forgotten about the deep chill and wet cold. His insulated long underwear helped some. His girlfriend Sherri had been surprised when he wrote asking for long underwear.

No one at home knew how cold it could be here during winter in the mountains. Of course he was the most envied man in his squad when the package arrived along with some stale chocolate chip cookies.

It was nearly a sacred duty to share any type of food packages from home. He shared the cookies, but refused all offers of barter, rent or lease of the thermal underwear. He had even refused the pleas of his best friend Doug Williams.

He and Williams had been friends since they sailed from San Diego, nearly a year ago. Doug had even tried to trade him the sacred panties.

O'Bryan smiled. The panties belonged to Doug's girlfriend. She had mailed them two months ago, along with a Polaroid photo of herself modeling them, in a care package. The black lacy things had been soaked in Chanel No. 5 and had "Doug" neatly stitched across the crotch. Williams often wore them over his head at night as mosquito netting. Doug sometimes rented the panties along with the Polaroid to other squad members on special occasions such as a birthday.

He looked down at the green luminous hands on his watch. Three more hours until dawn. God, he hated sitting out here alone. He wondered where the tiger had gone. He wondered if the N.V.A. would come tonight in a blaze of tracers and rocket fire. If they did he knew he would probably die.

The sole purpose of a listening post was to give a few minutes warning before an attack. Then he would be on his own, caught in the middle as the firefight exploded.

"What the hell am I doing here?" he whispered softly to himself. He wondered how a good Catholic boy from St. Mary's Academy in Washita, Oklahoma, had ended up on this godforsaken mountain half way around the world.

It was a simple question, but one which followed and haunted him. He wondered *Was it always like this? How many marines before me have sat in the dark and asked 'what the fuck am I doing here?'*

He did the only thing which brought relief in the terror of the night. He thought of home and a girl. O'Bryan had done this so many times before, it had become a ritual.

He began by clearing his mind of all thoughts. This was difficult and it took some time to reach that quiet spot within.

He then summoned the image of his house on South Eighth Street in Washita, Oklahoma. The tree lined streets and rolling yards were that fresh liquid green that only comes in April.

The image danced in the darkness in front of him. He stepped off his front porch and began to walk south down the street. He could smell crisp morning air. He tried to remember every detail of each friend's yard and home, as he walked south in his mind to Montana Street, then turned left.

He walked past "Hansen's," the neighborhood grocery store. He decided it should be Saturday morning. The parking lot of Hansen's was empty, and long morning shadows fell across the store front. He was going over to help her wash their family car, an old green Buick.

He finally came to her house on the corner and walked up the sidewalk to her front door. There were flowers blooming in the flower bed. Before he could knock, the white screen door opened and she stepped out.

She was wearing her favorite old blue T-shirt and a pair of cut-off white Levi's shorts. she stepped towards him and put her arms around his waist.

Sherri Langham at five feet, four inches and 105 pounds was a beautiful petite package to behold. He held her in his mind and she pressed her head against his chest.

Her auburn hair gleamed with reddish brown highlights in the morning sun. He smelled the fragrance of her hair mingled with the scent of her favorite perfume. Most of all he felt the softness of her pressed against him. He loved no thing or person in the world as he loved her.

A dull gray haze began to appear around him. Her image gradually grew dim and then disappeared as the night gave way to the morning fog. He tried to bring her back again in his mind, but she was gone.

He shivered and realized he was cold as the warmth of her died away. He had not seen her since his leave after boot camp a year and a half ago. His greatest fear was that some night he would not be able to remember her face or her smell. He would then be alone with no refuge in the night.

The morning fog brought reality with it. In ten more minutes it would be light enough to move back up to the relative safety and luxury of the squad bunker.

In the dingy mist, grimmer memories of home came

to him. The house he had thought of in the night was no longer his home. It had been repossessed by the mortgage company after his leave from boot camp. He could not blame the mortgage company. He and his sister had been abandoned by their parents and the loss of the house had been an anticlimax to his family's disintegration.

Drugs and alcohol had already burned the life from within the house. The mortgage company only took a shell. The same inferno now burned within him and had driven him here. He quickly dismissed these thoughts. Some things were too painful consider even in the daylight.

He longed for a cigarette and a hot cup of c-ration coffee. He stood stiffly and shouldered the P.R.C. 25 radio. He took one last look around and then began to trudge up the slippery hillside. He had survived another L.P. and another night. It seemed that for each step forward, he slipped two steps backwards. He slipped and fell forwards twice, and landed flat on his face both times. He had managed to nearly cover his poncho in mud. The edge of the perimeter was still hidden by the fog, but he knew he was getting close. He could hear fragments of voices in the thick mist above.

He stopped and called the C.P. on the radio to alert them that he was coming in. More than one marine had been killed while returning to his own lines.

As an extra precaution, for that ten percent who never get the word when it was passed, he would set off a green star cluster flare. This was the signal for friendlies approaching.

He reached into the deep side pocket of his jungle utility pants, and pulled out a foot long silver metal tube.

The men called them pop up flares. He pulled the metal cap off the top of the flare and placed it loosely over the bottom. He then slapped the bottom of the tube with the palm of his hand. This set off an ignition charge with a loud pop. Three bright green burning spheres shot seventy-five feet in the air. It always reminded O'Bryan of the Roman candle fireworks he and friends would set off on the Fourth of July. He watched the star clusters burn out and worried that the marines above him might not see them in the fog.

He took five more steps up the hill. Gunfire erupted immediately in front of him. He dove and flattened out in the mud. Bullets cracked over his head and an M60 machine gun opened up in ten-round bursts somewhere to his left. Each firefight has a rhythm and melody all its own. O'Bryan found this one was incomplete.

There was no answering chorus of AK-47s, which had a deeper report than the M16s. He then heard the unmistakable gravel voice of Sgt. Alvarez above.

"Cease fire you dumb motherfuckers." The command was repeated down the line, "Cease fire, cease fire." O'Bryan's hand shook as he grabbed the radio handset.

"L.P. Charley to Pine Pole Charley, what the hell is going on up there?"

"Pine Pole Charley to L.P. Charley, it's OK now, come on up," came the reply.

"Roger I'm coming in now," answered O'Bryan.

"Assholes trying to kill me," he muttered under his breath as he struggled the final thirty meters to the perimeter.

O'Bryan finally saw the barbed wire and trench line of the perimeter. He had unknowingly drifted to his right in the fog, and was surprised to see he had nearly walked around to the opposite side of the hill. He was greeted by the six foot five, lean black figure of a machine gunner in second squad named Highfield.

"Over here man," shouted Highfield, pointing to an entrance through the wire. O'Bryan walked through while Highfield held the wire to one side. "You better get your ass in here man, there's a tiger loose."

"No shit," said O'Bryan. "I saw him up close and personal last night." O'Bryan paused as he stepped over the trench line. "What the hell was all the shooting about? I nearly got blown away out there. Didn't you guys see the green star cluster?" Highfield leaned against a sandbagged bunker wall.

"Was that you that set off the flare? Well you spooked that cat over there," he pointed in the general direction of the trash dump. "A brother in first squad saw him and opened up with a sixteen. Said that cat had dug up two N.V.A. and a can of ham and lima beans."

Highfield paused and lit up a cigarette, then continued. "I don't know why everybody else started shootin'. If that cat ate them ham and lima beans he ain't got much time to live anyway."

O'Bryan now lit up his own cigarette and pulled deeply on it. He noted twenty fresh 7.62mm casings, obviously from Highfield's machine gun on the ground. He looked at Highfield.

"Did they hit the cat?"

"Hell no, that bad cat took of like an F-4 into the fog headed back down the hill. The Sarge is gonna be mad too. He said that if there was any shootin', there better be a dead pussy out here."

O'Bryan turned and walked towards the C.P. bunker. "I gotta get some chow and some sleep man. Better get rid of those shell casings. See you later."

O'Bryan turned in his radio at the C.P. and walked over to the south side of the hill to third squad's bunker. He pulled off the mud-covered poncho and spread it over the top of the sandbagged roof.

All the other squad members were in various stages of preparing their individual c-ration breakfasts. They were sitting and kneeling over the little brown boxes of canned food which comprised the daily diet of grunts.

To an outsider the marines would have appeared filthy. Each man had open sores at various places on his body, as a result of being constantly wet for the last two months. O'Bryan observed nothing unusual at all. He felt safe and at ease for the first time since he had left the squad last night.

These men were now his family. He walked over and squatted down squeezing into the rough semicircle of his squad. Each one knew the other in an elemental way that no one else would ever know them.

Most of them had been with the squad for at least nine months. The intensity of life in combat had compressed them into one persona. One night in a hole with a man here was equal to a year with him under normal circumstances.

They had all been stripped of any sort of pretense with each other. They shared each other's joys, sorrows, hopes, dreams and deaths. They had viewed each other's faces and saw their own souls laid bare and vulnerable, sprawled in rice paddies and flattened by fear along jungle trails.

They knew that their survival depended completely on each other. It was the sort of knowledge about one's self and others that few people ever learn, and produced a rare humility among them. There were no heroes here, just young men trying to become old men.

"O'Bryan!" a voice shouted from a bunker doorway. He looked up and saw a brown box of C-rations flying towards him. He reached with both hands and snatched the box in midair. Doug Williams emerged from the darkness of the doorway and smiled a crooked smile at him. "I saved you some scrambled eggs and ham." Williams stood about five-eleven with a slim athletic build. His sandy brown hair fell over his forehead above dark blue eyes. In two months he would turn twenty-one

"Thanks," said O'Bryan. Williams walked over and sat down next to him.

"Isn't this great?" O'Bryan looked up from his green cans of food and stared intently at Williams.

"Well it depends on what you mean. Are you talking about the food, the war, or just life in general?" Williams held his hands palms up to the sky. "No rain, no rain."

O'Bryan looked up. He was so exhausted, he hadn't even noticed the rain had stopped for the first time in recent memory.

The sky was still heavy and gray, but the rain had stopped. Williams looked blankly into space. His voice assumed a soft nearly prayerful tone. "You know, maybe the resupply chopper can come in today, if it clears just a little."

"Yeah," answered O'Bryan in the same wistful tone.

"Maybe we might even get some mail." O'Bryan's head

dropped down and he looked at his food.

"Don't get your hopes up Doug. Even if a chopper does make it in today, it'll be loaded down with ammo and C rats."

Williams now shook his head and focused his thoughts. "How was the L.P. last night? I heard you had a visitor."

"Well it was interesting. A tiger nosed around me, I froze my ass off in the rain, and Highfield, over in third squad nearly blew me away when I came in."

Williams smiled at him. "Other than that did anything happen?"

O'Bryan laughed, "No, just another glorious night in the Nam."

Williams was busy now, making a C-ration stove. He used a small C-ration opener to make a row of triangular holes around the bottom edge of an empty can. He looked up from his task. "Look at it this way: you can sleep in the bunker all day, while the rest of us bail out the trench and fill sandbags. Alvarez has already passed the word on working parties."

O'Bryan found it nearly impossible to stay depressed around Doug Williams. He was one of those people who seemed to find an upside to any circumstance. In combat, Williams was rock-solid with a composure that belied his carefree attitude. He and Williams had come through for each other with their lives on the line. They were bonded together in a friendship built on total trust.

Doug was from Anaheim, California. He had been a freshman at U.C.L.A. until too many hours of partying had dropped his grade point average. The draft board was notified and he received his notice. To the dismay of his entire family, he chose to serve two years in the Marines.

One of Doug's fondest memories, which he had described in great detail to O'Bryan, was a two-day going away party held at different locations across southern California. O'Bryan thought of him as a true free spirit. Even ten months in Vietnam had not seemed to faze Williams's outlook on life.

O'Bryan finished making his tin-can stove. He held out his hand. "Doug pass me some C-4." Williams reached into a green pack and pulled out a one-pound white brick of C-4 high explosive. The government supplied them with small green tablets known as "heat tabs," for warming the cans of C-rations.

Grunts however, found that these slow-burning green tabs left much to be desired. They gave off an unpleasant smell, which sometimes tainted the food, and were always in short supply.

Some unknown grunt inventor discovered that a marble size ball of C-4 used in the same manner and lit with a match, would prepare one can of C-ration food perfectly.

It was a safe procedure as long as the stove can was properly ventilated. A few new men sometimes produced an exploding can of ham and lima beans, but they eventually got the knack of it. It was another little trick you learned, if you survived long enough.

O'Bryan took the block of C-4 and pinched off a small amount. It had the same consistency as cookie dough. The one-pound block he held was equivalent to twelve sticks of TNT. He rolled the dab of C-4 into a small ball.

"John, did I tell you my sister is sending another care package?"

"No, what did you ask for?"

"She's sending a new bottle of hot sauce, an onion, canned peaches and three sticks of smoked sausage."

O'Bryan wrapped his arms around his stomach. "A squad feast."

Williams again looked at the low gray sky. "If the weather holds maybe it'll come today."

"Hope so," said O'Bryan. "I could sure use a letter from Sherri."

O'Bryan ate his food quickly and then heated a can of water. He removed a small packet of instant coffee from the brown plastic condiments package that came with the C-rations, and emptied it into the water. He took his hot coffee and leaned back with a cigarette. This was the moment he longed for all night.

The fog had begun to lift, and he surveyed the lush green mountains and valleys.

"You know, Doug, if there wasn't a war going on, this place would be beautiful."

"Well if there wasn't a war, John, we wouldn't be sittin' here looking at it."

"Hey, when this is over let's take all the money we saved, come back here and build a cabin over by the old French plantation at Lang Vei."

"You mean over there east of the base where the Special Forces and CIA spooks are?"

"Sure, why not? We could get us some Montagnard women and become coffee plantation owners."

"You been over here too long O'Bryan. The Montagnard men look better than the women anyway. You're starting to go native on me."

O'Bryan placed a finger at each corner of his eyes and

pushed until they became narrow slits.

"What makes you say that, Yankee Imperialist pig?"

Williams shook his head and picked up the trash from his meal.

"Go get some sleep. You're really gettin' squirrely. I'll wake you if we get some mail."

O'Bryan gathered his trash and handed it to Williams. "Here, as long as you're headed over to the trash dump."

Williams reluctantly took the box of trash.

"I'll take it, but if I see your tiger friend from last night, I'll tell him where you're at."

"I don't think he'll be interested in me," replied O'Bryan. "From what I hear, he may have developed a taste for ripe N.V.A. last night."

Williams frowned, "You're a sick man, go to bed."

O'Bryan lay down in a corner of the squad bunker on his air mattress. He pulled his poncho liner over him and thought about the last twenty-four hours. It had been, as he told Doug, a typical day. Hours on end of boredom, broken by moments of sheer terror.

He drifted off with a question in his mind. Was he just getting used to life here, or had he nearly grown to like it here? The thought disturbed him, but not enough to keep him awake.

While O'Bryan slept, some twenty miles from his bunker, over one thousand North Vietnamese trucks wound down Route 9 from North Vietnam into Laos. The trucks were well camouflaged and drove at wide-spaced intervals, as protection from the ever present danger of air strikes. The trucks carried two elite N.V.A. divisions. The 325 C and 304th divisions, who had a combined strength of nearly 20,000 men.

They were well equipped with Soviet weapons and most were seasoned combat veterans. These men were following orders of General Vo Nguyen Giap, the man who had trapped and annihilated 10,000 French troops fourteen years earlier at Dien Bein Phu.

Already, scout elements of the 325 C division were approaching a hill only 800 meters from O'Bryan's squad. A nearly invisible element of hand picked North Vietnamese soldiers preceded the main force.

CHAPTER TWO

Lieutenant Vinh Nguyen was the leader of a nine-man team sent to scout the hills to the north and northwest of the Marine base at Khe Sanh.

He paused in the thick undergrowth to listen. Nguyen was from a small farming village about twenty miles southwest of Hanoi. The men of his village had been farming there for over two hundred years.

His father had broken the long tradition by becoming a soldier. He had followed the revolutionary Ho Chi Minh in the late 1930s. He fought the French soldiers and then the hated Japanese invaders, for his country's independence.

The Japanese had driven the French out, and won control of the cities. But Ho Chi Minh and his Viet Minh controlled the countryside.

In those days the Americans were their friends. They sent rifles, ammunition and medical supplies to fight the hated Japanese invaders.

The Japanese soldiers were brutal and their prowess as jungle fighters was well known. But when they ventured outside the safe confines of cities and roads, the Viet Minh had cut them to pieces with their slash and run tactics.

Nguyen's father had told him many stories about the wars. How everyone rejoiced when they learned that the Japanese had surrendered to the Americans. The people waited for the Americans to come and take the Japanese from the cities. Instead, the Americans had betrayed them.

The imperialist French returned, and as a further

insult, the pompous French allowed the Japanese to keep their guns and police the cities for them.

His father had been with the forces who finally overran the French at Dien Bien Phu and put an end to their oppression. Now Vinh Nguyen son of Lam Nguyen, would help drive the Americans from his country and then unite the people in the south with their brothers in the north.

His orders were to scout the hills around the Marine base at Khe Sanh and determine the strength and disposition of the Americans. He and his men had received special training from Russian advisors in weapons and explosives.

They had recruited a local mountain tribesman named Lot, who knew the area well. Lot now walked ten meters in front of him, in the dense undergrowth of a mountain valley.

The Americans regularly mined and bombed this valley, because it was the most direct approach to the base from across the Laotian border.

Vinh Nguyen did not trust Lot. Lot had also worked for the American Special Forces and CIA at Lang Vei. He had been recruited by Trung Ly, the team's political officer, in a village just inside Laos.

The political officer had simply promised Lot more food and money. The mountain people were strange. They seemed to have no loyalty to anyone and considered anyone who farmed and lived on the low lands as inferior. They were mountain hunters and fought for no one but themselves.

The French had simply called them Montagnards which meant mountain people. Nguyen knew there were differences in the tribes, but did not know what they were. He did know that he did not trust this one. But Lot claimed to know the area, and particularly the hills around Khe Sanh, so he had not objected to Trung Ly's idea. His unit, like all North Vietnamese units, was comprised of three-man cells. Each unit was assigned a political cadre who was responsible for the unit's morale and made sure the party guidelines were followed. Lt. Nguyen, while out-ranking Trung Ly, knew it would not be good to oppose his decisions on such matters.

They moved at a slow pace because Lot stopped often to eat and lighten his heavy pack filled with rice and dried fruit. Nguyen was not happy with the slow pace, but he knew that it was better to keep Lot full of food and happy.

He looked up to see that Lot had stopped again. But this time Lot motioned for the rest of the team to come forward. Nguyen approached cautiously. It would not be the first time a mountain man had walked North Vietnamese into an ambush.

When he was even with Lot, he could see he was smiling. He pointed to a flat spot in some grass below on the hillside. Nguyen could see the tail fin assembly of a dud 250-pound bomb sticking out of the dirt.

He had taken a special interest in these American bombs. A bomb identical to this one had landed just outside his village ten months ago.

His father, mother and two small cousins had been visiting their small village shrine. The bomb had blasted them and the small Buddhist shrine to bits and pieces. He already knew that he must dig this one up and return it to the Americans.

*   *   *

O'Bryan awakened and sat up quickly. His right hand reached out for his rifle. The bunker was cool and dark. He listened in the darkness. His mind began to clear and update him with his surroundings.

He sat up startled and confused. The results of standing countless hours of night watches were taking a toll on him. Now he could never really sleep. He slipped instead into a nether region between conscious and unconscious. Upon rising he felt he was never really awake. He could no longer rest.

He looked at the glowing green hands of his watch. It was 5 p.m. He had been asleep for ten hours. He felt in the darkness for his pack, cartridge belt and canteen.

He knew there was only an hour of daylight left and the squad would be preparing their dinners soon.

He walked down the narrow aisle that separated the scattered bedding and gear on either side of the bunker, feeling his way along the mud floor. He pushed aside the poncho which hung over the bunker doorway and squinted into a gray hazy sunlight.

"Rise and shine, sweet pea." O'Bryan turned and saw Corporal Grayson, his squad leader, standing on the bunker roof above him. "You look like shit." O'Bryan pulled himself out of the five-foot trench, stretched and looked around.

"Did the chopper come in yet?"

"Suppose to be here any time," replied Grayson scanning the sky.

O'Bryan squatted on the ground and poured a handful of water from his canteen. He splashed the water on his face and dried himself with a dirty dark green towel that was wrapped around his pack. Next he rinsed his mouth with water and sprinkled some salt from a small square C-rat pack onto his toothbrush. Toothpaste was a luxury reserved for the rear echelon people.

Because of resupply problems, water was confined to drinking and cooking. None of the men had shaved in weeks. O'Bryan stripped down and checked himself for leeches. He grimaced at the smell of his own clothing. He stood 6'3" tall and now weighed 160 pounds. His skin seemed to have taken on a walnut stain during the last year, which sharply contrasted with blue eyes. He had celebrated his nineteenth birthday in June. During the last summer he had turned darker than some of the light-skinned black marines. His black hair hung greasy and matted over his ears. He yelled up at Grayson.

"Any leeches on my back?"

"You're clean. You know, O'Bryan, you're startin' to look more like a gook every day."

"Thanks Grayson," mumbled O'Bryan out of the corner of his mouth. He quickly pulled the thermal underwear and jungle utilities back on.

The distinctive chop of helicopter blades, faint but unmistakable, could be heard overhead. Every face on the hill tilted up to search the sky. Huey gunship dipped from the low hanging clouds and made two banking passes around the hill. A green smoke grenade popped on the makeshift mud landing zone, down the east slope of the hill.

Staff Sergeant Alvarez's voice boomed from the doorway of the command post bunker.

"All working parties to the L.Z., let's get that chopper

unloaded and out of here."

Men scurried from the trench line and bunkers to form a human chain from the C.P. bunker to the L.Z.

The CH-34 helicopter resembled a large green grasshopper with its big rounded nose and tapered body, as it sat down very tentatively, tail first in the mud. "Lets go second squad," shouted Grayson, and O'Bryan ran with the rest of the men to join the human chain to the L.Z.

The noise and wind from the helicopter was deafening. The copter pilot and copilot sat nervously exposed, high up in the cockpit. They kept the engine straining, ready to lift off at the first sign off trouble.

Five-gallon water cans were passed from the helicopter down the chain of men to the C.P., where all incoming supplies were stacked for distribution. Next came the boxes of C-rations, then ammunition. Finally, two red nylon mail bags were tossed from the helicopter.

Because of the noise, the first two explosions went nearly unnoticed. A marine stacking supplies next to O'Bryan felt something like bee stings on his left shoulder and arm. He reached around with his right hand to brush whatever it was away. He felt something warm and sticky on his hand and saw that it was drenched in blood. He began to scream and yell, but the helicopter drowned his voice. He dropped to the ground, and tried to pull off the shirt, but his hands only clutched at his chest.

O'Bryan turned to hand the man another box of C-rations, but he was not there. The box dropped to the ground. He looked down and saw the contorted face of the marine writhing on the ground. The man had pulled open his shirt and had what appeared to be a thousand tiny pin holes across his left shoulder, arm and chest. Blood poured from each small hole.

Over the din of the helicopter's noise, O'Bryan recognized Alvarez's gravely voice, "Incoming!"

The next two 60mm mortar rounds landed nearly on top of Alvarez, who stood beside the C.P. bunker. One of his arms was immediately severed and the blast tossed him on the bunker roof. The helicopter quickly lifted off, dipping down the north side of the hill. A Huey gunship appeared from nowhere and fired 4.2-inch rockets randomly into a nearby hillside.

O'Bryan was running bent three feet off the ground at full speed. Two more mortar rounds impacted somewhere behind him. He dove head first to cover the last six feet to the trench. He tried to break the fall into the trench with his hands and jammed his left wrist. He rolled on the bottom of the trench and scrambled down the line to the bunker. He ripped the poncho off the doorway, stepped inside and emerged in thirty seconds with his helmet, flak jacket, M16 rifle and a bandoleer of thirty-two magazines.

Soon the whole squad was strung down the trench line, rifles at the ready, awaiting an enemy ground assault. Moaning and cries of "Corpsman!" could be heard behind them towards the command post area.

They waited in the trench for two hours. Listening posts were sent out. The mountain darkness dropped suddenly on them. Still they waited, looking out, searching for movement in the night.

Some whispers spread down the trench. Alvarez was dead, so were Jordan the radio operator, and Wilkins, the man who had stood next to O'Bryan. Each man stood silent, in his own state of mourning.

The platoon would miss Alvarez. He had been a rock.

A twenty-three-year veteran of the old corps. The bravest man O'Bryan had ever seen under fire. Alvarez had joined the Marines at age seventeen in 1945. He had lost three toes and the tip of his nose to frostbite in the bloody march from the Chosin reservoir in Korea. Sometimes while standing watch in the trench, Alvarez would suddenly appear next to a man who was fighting sleep. In a low whisper he would tell a story from that frozen hell.

He had survived all that to die on this stinking hill, thought O'Bryan. The platoon would demand retribution, but it would not come tonight.

Finally the word came to go to fifty percent watch. O'Bryan, Williams, and Halpin returned to the squad bunker, while the rest of the squad stood fast.

Corporal Grayson waited for them at the bunker entrance. He had carried water and a case of C-rations from the C.P. to the bunker. "Get the poncho back up so I can use the flashlight." O'Bryan and Williams picked up the poncho and tucked the corners under the sandbags over the doorway.

Once inside Grayson switched his flashlight on. Each man removed his gear and dropped it at his sleeping spot. Grayson sat the case of C-rations down in a vacant corner. "We eat cold tonight," said Grayson.

O'Bryan noticed there were dark red spots on the front of the brown cardboard case. No one seemed to be hungry. Grayson reached into the big side pocket of his jungle pants and pulled out a stack of letters. "Williams, you got a package at the C.P., but I couldn't carry it all. Run up there and get it."

"All right," replied Williams, who was already on his way out. Grayson shuffled through the letters, holding the flashlight under his arm.

"Halpin," he said handing two letters to the little radio man from West Virginia.

"O'Bryan."

"Thanks Grayson," said O'Bryan and reached for his letter.

He sat down and took off his boots. He knew in four hours he would be back in the trench while the others rested.

Williams came in with a two-foot-long package. "My sister came through," he beamed. O'Bryan leaned back on one elbow.

He pulled a candle from the bottom of his pack. There was only an inch left of his last candle. He used it sparingly, but there was no greater occasion than a letter from her.

He lit the candle and looked at the light blue envelope with her beautiful flowing script. She had addressed it to L/Cpl. Johnny M. O'Bryan. Johnny, he thought. No one but his family and friends at home called him Johnny. Not even Doug called him Johnny. He would have gladly paid $500, just to hear her voice say his name.

He smiled, Johnny was from another life. He didn't know when Johnny had died, but he knew the boy no longer existed. He lay somewhere discarded between his dreams and the reality of war.

He carefully opened the envelope with a bayonet. Her letters were such fragile things and had to last for so long. The squad had not received any mail in over three weeks. He had read her last letter eight times and it was dirty and smudged from the rereading.

He devoured the first paragraph and felt as if his

stomach had turned inside out. He didn't want to keep reading but some morbid need to know why, kept him going on.

She said there was someone else and that it was not anyone's fault. She would always love him and wanted to be friends, but she just couldn't be engaged to him anymore. They had always been honest with each other and she had to tell him the way she felt.

He dropped the letter on the muddy bunker floor and blew out the candle. He went to the bunker doorway and out into the trench. In a moment he vomited the remains of his C-ration breakfast. His ears rang and he gasped for breath.

"You OK, John?" He felt a hand on his shoulder and knew it was Williams.

"I'll be OK, just need some air."

"I'll get you some water." Williams returned with a canteen and an entrenching tool. He handed the canteen to O'Bryan and covered the vomit with three shovels full of dirt. O'Bryan could only see his dark outline.

"Thanks Doug."

"No big deal, you feel better?"

"No," sighed O'Bryan. "My girl just wrote me to say so long, friend. She's got someone else."

"No shit," said Williams. "She got another guy?"

"That's what it sounds like."

"How long since you saw her?"

"About a year and a half."

"Well at least you weren't married or anything. I've seen a lot of married guys get those letters over here. It drives them crazy. Some of them go out and try to get their ass blown away. But you're not that stupid."

"No," came out of O'Bryan in a small voice. "I just kind of want to be alone."

"Sure thing, John. My sister sent all the stuff I asked for. The guys are wantin' to divide up the sausages."

"Go ahead, I'll be there in a few minutes."

Williams turned and walked back down the trench to the bunker entrance.

O'Bryan stood alone in the darkness. He rubbed his sore wrist and wept as quietly as he could. He did not hate the girl, but he feared having no refuge in the night. He looked up and saw the moon flutter between the clouds. A cool mist covered his face. He thought that he might be sick again and that he would never love another person.

Later he walked back to the bunker. He found the letter folded and back in its envelope, lying on his blanket. He laid down and wondered if there was a God. He decided if there was, He had forgotten him, or maybe He died, along with Johnny.

Lt. Nguyen ate half a ball of rice with two dried strips of fish, and washed it down with a gulp of water. He sat on the ground next to a five-foot-deep hole, camouflaged by thick vines and leaves. Lot had the first watch, but he would not sleep until Lot had been relieved. He could not see Lot, but knew he sat in a clump of vines six feet away, feasting on dried fruit.

The day had been a disappointment, he thought. They had waited for the helicopter to touch down before launching the six 60mm mortar rounds in rapid succession. The first two rounds had landed too far up the hill and the helicopter had escaped. They did not wait to see the other rounds land. They had barely gotten in their holes when the gunship had opened fire.

The rockets landed nowhere near them, but Lot had been slow and the gunship might have seen him. He counted on the marines' own reputation for aggressiveness. They knew a mortar team was nearby. They would come looking.

There appeared to be a platoon on the hill, from what he could see with his binoculars. Tomorrow he would note the bunker positions on the map he was drawing.

He pulled his arms tight around his knees. The night was pitch black and his mind wandered first to thoughts of his village, then to a girl he had met while being trained in Hanoi.

She had been in a bomb disposal class with him. She was shy and quiet. He had been immediately smitten by her. There were no women like her in his home village of Thuy Bo. She was very pretty, along with being smart and brave, he thought.

The shortage of men had opened up these dangerous and technical jobs to women. She had been one of the first to volunteer. Only later did he learn why.

American bombs had also taken members of her family. The women had been trained to work in the Hanoi area, so that more men could be sent to the great struggle in the south.

His hand patted the plastic bag in his breast pocket. It contained the only letter he had received from her, and a photo they had made together before he left Hanoi. The photo had been taken in a small shop by an old man. They stood together in front of a painted blue sky background, wearing their khaki uniforms and smiling proudly. Her long black hair was pulled up on her head and a shy smile crept across her delicate face.

It was against regulations for him to carry this letter and photo. He was always very careful to see that Trung Ly never saw them, because Trung Ly would certainly report him. Even so, he would never part with them.

He patted the photo in his pocket and leaned back on the thick vines. Soon it would be Trung Ly's watch and he could get some sleep. Trung Ly had argued strongly against letting the Americans know they were in the area. He had agreed with Ly that their mission was to scout and report, and the mission came first. But they were also soldiers. If they could kill twenty or thirty Americans, they were cowards not to do so.

Trung Ly had finally relented, but only on the condition that there would be no risk of discovery and capture. Nguyen had seen Ly writing in a notebook that only the political cadre were allowed to keep. He nearly laughed to himself. They would both be very lucky if they survived long enough for Trung Ly to make his report. Maybe the Americans would come tomorrow.

CHAPTER THREE

The following day the weather held and the helicopters returned around 9 a.m. as the fog had begun to lift. O'Bryan and the rest of the squad watched from the cover of the trench as two helicopters took turns landing.

The company commander of B Co., Capt. Hudson, dashed off to the first helicopter as soon as it touched down. Three green body bags and four wounded marines were quickly loaded on the chopper and it immediately lifted off. The next helicopter touched down with the remainder of the prior day's aborted supply run.

There was no mortar fire today. The squad members watched as Lt. Henderson and Capt. Hudson walked up the hill from the L.Z. to the platoon Command Post bunker.

The men of second squad pulled themselves up on the side of the trench line and resumed cleaning their weapons. Williams and O'Bryan sat next to each other. On the ground between them was a green towel on which they spread out the parts of their M16 rifles. Williams held out his hand. "Pass me the bore brush and Hoppies. What do you think the skipper's doing up here?"

O'Bryan handed over the bottle of cleaning solvent and brush. "Well we're about due to rotate back down to the base. I bet they want us to pull a sweep around here before the new platoon takes over. See if we can find the N.V.A. that mortared us."

Williams considered this for a moment. "Those assholes are probably back in Laos by now. Man, humpin' those hills in the mud could be a bitch, but I sure would like to get my sights on one of those gooks, get some payback."

O'Bryan did not answer; he seemed preoccupied. He finished cleaning his rifle in silence, then quickly reassembled the field-stripped M16. He tried the action once and sprang to his feet.

"Where you goin'?" asked Williams, not looking up.

"Up to the C.P., got to check on something."

"Tell 'em we want a raise and better working conditions," Williams yelled at O'Bryan's back.

He walked quickly to the C.P. bunker. He had not slept last night thinking over what he was about to do. He stopped at the bunker entrance and took a deep breath. What the hell, he thought and stepped inside.

Lt. Henderson and Capt. Hudson were bent over an ammo crate table, next to the platoon radio, studying a map. O'Bryan stood silently a few feet away, waiting for them to acknowledge him.

Capt. Hudson pointed with his index finger. "Your platoon will sweep through the valley. You shove off in the morning at o6oo hours. Second Platoon will fly in and set up positions along this ridge line. First Platoon will be here this afternoon. They will relieve you and man your positions here on the hill. They will also serve as our reserve force. When the patrol is over your platoon and Second Platoon will sweep back to Khe Sanh. Any questions?"

"No, Skipper. Any intelligence about opposition?" Henderson asked as he looked up and noticed O'Bryan.

"None," replied the Captain, "but Division said infrared flight scans show some heavy troop movements across the border in Laos."

Lt. Henderson nodded thoughtfully and looked up at O'Bryan. "What is it?"

O'Bryan shifted his weight nervously. "Sir, I want to fill out one of those forms to extend my tour."

O'Bryan was framed by hazy light from the bunker doorway. Lt. Henderson stepped around the Captain. "You thought this over?"

"Yes sir, I have."

"How long you been in-country now?"

"Ten months, sir."

"OK, have a seat outside, I'll be with you in a minute."

"Yes, sir." O'Bryan turned and walked out the bunker doorway.

Lt. Henderson turned back to his Captain. "It'll be slow going over this soggy ground."

"That's OK," he said, refolding his map. "This isn't a race. I want every square inch of that valley checked. I want the gun crew that killed Alvarez."

"You got it, Skipper."

O'Bryan sat on the ground with his back against the sandbagged C.P. wall. He mentally recited his reasons for extending. *I've got too much time left on my four-year enlistment. I'm gonna do two tours over here one way or another. I might as well get it over with all at once. Plus I'll get thirty days free leave and...*

"O'Bryan!" shouted Lt. Henderson from the bunker. "Come in here."

"Yes, sir," he replied, popping to his feet and walking inside the bunker doorway.

Henderson handed him a one-page type-written form. "Read this."

"Yes, sir." O'Bryan was too excited. He could not focus on the small print. He turned to read it in the light from the doorway. After a few seconds he looked up, having read only half the form. He turned and handed the paper back to Lt. Henderson, fighting to control the fear in his voice. "OK, sir."

Henderson sat down at the radio table and pulled a pen from his pocket. "What's your service number?"

"2136595."

"Sign here at the bottom, your payroll signature, and I'll witness it."

O'Bryan bent over the table and signed his name, then straightened up.

"When do you want your thirty days leave?"

"I don't know, sir, I really hadn't thought about that."

Capt. Hudson walked to Alvarez's vacant bunk and sat down. "Where are you taking your leave?"

"I haven't decided on that either, Captain."

Hudson lit a cigarette and offered one to O'Bryan. "Tell me, O'Bryan," Hudson paused as he handed him a Marlboro, "why are you extending? We don't get very many extendees from rifle companies."

"Well sir, I send all my money home to a savings account. I plan on using that and my G.I. Bill to go to college when my four years is up. Being a grunt is all I know how to do, and this is where I make the most money doing it."

"So you're extending for the extra combat pay?"

"Not just that, sir. I've lost some good friends over here, like Sgt. Alvarez. I figure the score's not even yet."

That seemed to satisfy the Captain. He nodded, stood, and offered his hand. "Good luck, son."

"Thank you, sir," replied O'Bryan, shaking the Captain's hand.

Lt. Henderson next shook O'Bryan's hand. "Glad you're staying for awhile, O'Bryan. We can used an experienced man. Let me know when you decide on your leave date."

"Yes sir." O'Bryan turned and ducked out the doorway.

"Good kid," said Hudson as he sat back down.

"They're all so young," replied Henderson. "I just hope he makes it."

Captain Hudson looked down at O'Bryan's extension form. "You know, I wish we didn't have these damned thirteen-month rotations. They ruin a unit's cohesion, and we constantly have to train green troops. I wish they didn't force that on us."

"I know, I'd rather they'd rotate whole units in and out. It would make for better morale and in the long run I think the experience factor would reduce casualties."

Hudson dropped his cigarette on the floor. "God damned D.O.D. people are running this thing into the ground with all their silly-ass rules." He ground the cigarette out with his boot on the dirt floor. "Give me O'Bryan's extension, I'll turn it in at Regiment when I get back."

O'Bryan felt light-headed as he walked back to the squad bunker. He smiled to himself. *I wonder if I just signed my own death certificate? Who gives a shit? I think*

I'll go to Australia.

Williams and Cory, the squad machine gunner, sat next to the trench checking some linked ammo for the squad's M60 machine gun. O'Bryan squatted down next to them.

"Better make sure you got a good spare barrel and plenty of ammo, Cory."

"You expecting some shit O'Bryan?"

"We're pullin' a sweep tomorrow. Just heard it from the skipper at the C.P."

"Shit," said Williams and Cory in unison.

Williams looked over at O'Bryan. "What were you doin' over at the C.P.?"

"Just signed up for a trip to Australia."

"Sure, O'Bryan, you already been on R&R."

Williams's eyes narrowed. "Wait a minute. You didn't go and do something really stupid, did you? We just got ninety days left over here."

O'Bryan looked at both of them, shrugged his shoulders.

Williams stood up. "If you extended you're the dumbest son of bitch I've ever known."

Cory chimed in, "If you want to die so bad, why don't you just shoot yourself. But first sign over your G.I. insurance to the squad and we'll have a big party in your honor."

O'Bryan stood up, lifted his head and held out his arms. "This is my land, Cory. As soon as we get rid of all these gooks, I'm goin' to build a house here."

"That's it, Williams, your partner gone nuts. The boy needs to talk to one of those Navy shrinks."

O'Bryan ignored the remark, dropped into the trench

and walked towards the bunker. "I'm going to get some rest. The skipper said we're jumpin' off at 0600."

Cory looked at Williams and shook his head.

"Why would anyone want to stay over here a day longer than he has to?"

Williams folded a belt of machine gun ammo back into a canvas carrying bag. He looked up at Cory. "I think O'Bryan just really doesn't care. Maybe he thinks there's nowhere else he belongs."

Cory looked over the gun and gazed at the mountains around them. "That's a scary thought. No one belongs here. Either they were born here, sent here, or they absolutely got nowhere else to go."

Williams stood up. "You mean if Mom and Dad couldn't get 'em out of the draft or into college or the reserves?"

"That's right. Just remember you had it made, Williams. You could still be back in the States runnin' around with little long-haired girls and protestin' the war, if you hadn't screwed up."

"I let my big sister take care of all that, she's the protester in the family."

"Your sister a hippie?"

"Naw, she just doesn't like the war."

"I can dig that."

"You know, Cory, if I was a gook, I'd probably be out there shootin' at our sorry asses too. You got to give the little bastards credit, standin' up to air strikes and artillery. They got balls."

"Yeah, I think about that every time I put a machine gun round through one of 'em."

"You're cold blooded, Corey."

"It's a war, baby. It don't make a shit who's wrong or right. You sort that out later. The winners make the rules. If we'd lost the Second World War, they would have tried Eisenhower and what's his name..."

"Churchill."

"Yeah, but we won so what we did was right."

"You mean the main thing is you got to win."

"That's it."

"My sister would say that was very Machiavellian."

"What's that?"

"Machiavelli was a guy, thought just like you do."

"He must be a cool dude then."

"He's real cool, he's dead."

"He must've screwed up then."

Williams lit up a cigarette and decided the conversation had gone on about as far as he cared for it to. "Well, I got to go talk O'Bryan out of this extending crap. He's just upset over his girl droppin' him. It's not legal until it gets approved. He can still withdraw the request."

"I hope so. I kind of like O'Bryan. Hate to see him go home in a body bag or you know, like second base."

"You know, you got a way with words Cory. Why don't you tell him that."

Williams collected his rifle and cleaning gear, then jumped into the trench and walked down to the bunker.

O'Bryan sat on the bunker floor with his candle studying the letter from Sherri Langham.

"Stop reading that shit. You should have it memorized by now. That's what all this extension stuff is about. You're just upset over the letter. Hey, just because you're pissed off at the girl is no reason to try and get yourself killed."

O'Bryan didn't reply, but folded the letter neatly and

put it in a clear plastic bag with his other letters from her.

"I'm goin' to write my sister a letter right now."

Williams pulled some stationery and a candle from his pack. "I'm going to tell her all about you and how you're my partner. I'll have her get two or three of her friends to write you and send along a picture of themselves. These are nice little Southern California coeds. Buddy, the world is full of girls. By the time we rotate back to the States we'll have a handful to check out."

Williams settled down on the dirt floor next to O'Bryan and began to write.

"Sounds good to me," O'Bryan conceded.

"O.K., but you tell the lieutenant you changed your mind and you're not extending."

"What's that got to do with it?"

"Look, if you don't, I'm not going to expose my sister or her friends to some crazy suicidal asshole. Come on, we'll find you a new girl and then go back home together. We'll have a blast, man. A major homecoming event."

"OK, OK, I'll tell the lieutenant tomorrow. But you know they're going to send me back again sometime. I just got too much time to do in the Corps. It's different for you, you only got drafted for two years. I'm in this thing until 1969."

"I know, but at least make 'em send you back here. Who knows, maybe they'll send you on a Med. Cruise or somethin'."

"I wish. You know there's only three kinds of marines right now. The ones coming over here, the ones going back and the ones that already been shot."

"Well you'll never find out unless you give it a chance."

"All right, all right, you win, I said I'll talk to the

lieutenant tomorrow."

Corporal Grayson entered the bunker and paused for a moment to adjust to the dim light. "You guys finish up your letters and come outside. We're going to draw food and ammo. We shove off at 0600 tomorrow. Get all your gear together and be ready to saddle up. First Platoon is going to double up with us tonight, so store your packs in the trench line."

Williams looked up from his stationery. "OK we'll be out in just a minute." Grayson turned and went back out into the trench. "All right, O'Bryan, what color of hair do you prefer, blond, brunette, or redhead? I got to give my sister some basic information to go on."

"O'Bryan rubbed his chin thoughtfully for a moment. "If this is a California girl I better go with a blond."

"Check," Williams replied. "Now how about age?"

"Oh I don't know, say eighteen to twenty-one."

"They're all eighteen to twenty-one. You're nineteen, right?"

"Yep."

"I'll say we prefer nineteen. How tall?"

"We, I thought this was for me?"

"It is, but of course I'm going to have to screen some of these letters. Now how tall?"

"I don't care, use your best judgement. You sure your sister will go along with this?"

Williams paused and put the tip of his pen to his teeth. "No problem, my sister hates the war, but she's crazy about me. This is kind of fun. Sort of like ordering out of a catalogue."

O'Bryan smiled, "Sorta Sears for the lovelorn."

The platoon was up at 0530 and ate in the darkness.

At 6 a.m. they began to file off the hill into the fog and jungle. They moved in a column with a ten-meter interval between each man. The only sound was the loud click of rifle bolts as each man locked and loaded as he left the perimeter. The dawn light made them silhouettes to each other as they struggled over a 900-foot hill and approached the valley at a slow cautious pace. Daylight gradually revealed low-hanging clouds, but there was no rain.

No one spoke. They fanned out into a wedge formation on the cue of Cpl. Grayson's hand signal. The squad had swept through a hundred similar valleys, and each man knew his role.

Grayson walked about twenty meters behind the point man with his radio man, Halpin, one step behind him.

Taylor had the point. He was the best point man O'Bryan had ever seen. Taylor was from Georgia and spoke with a slow thick southern accent. He had told O'Bryan that the trick was to see the smallest detail that didn't belong. He seemed to be able to sense trip wires and had an uncanny ability to see what could not be seen by anyone else.

Some of the men said it was luck. Some said it was ESP. O'Bryan and Williams agreed that whatever it was, it worked. His movements were fluid, precise and silent.

When the lieutenant put Taylor on point, the whole platoon knew it was serious. His unique talents were saved for the most deadly of occasions. He was the best they had.

O'Bryan watched as Taylor's wispy figure paused, then eased over a small hill in front of them. O'Bryan and Williams followed on the right flank of the wedge formation, with a fifteen-meter interval between them. He felt an itchy sting on his right calf and knew he had picked up a leech.

He bent down on one knee and laid his M16 next to him. Williams disappeared over the crest of the hill to his left front. O'Bryan pulled up his pant leg and saw a two-inch brown leech sticking out from under the top of his sock. The rest of the platoon passed by on either side of him. He fumbled with a plastic container which held his C-ration cigarettes and matches.

He lit the cigarette and took two deep drags then touched the red hot tip to the back of the leech's head. The shiny brown blob dropped to the ground and blood oozed from the small circular bite. He took some C-ration toilet paper and dabbed at the blood. Finally he took a small piece of the paper and stuck it to the bite to stop the bleeding.

He stood and hurried to catch up with the platoon. When he topped the hill he could see them spread out on the small valley below. The tops of their helmets formed an arrowhead which snaked through the tall grass. He knew Taylor was in front of his squad which was the point of the arrow, but he could not see him. Taylor refused to wear a helmet when he walked point. He told O'Bryan it ruined his hearing. Taylor must have stopped. Everyone below stood stone still. He decided to take advantage of the halt to close the distance to his squad.

The six-foot-high expanse of elephant grass rolled and swayed like a huge green ocean swell. He paused, and knew why Taylor had stopped. The only sound came from the wind gently rustling each giant blade against the other.

The huge explosion came with no warning. One instant O'Bryan was walking and the next a shock wave pounded him backwards to the ground. The elephant grass was flattened for a moment and the air was filled with thick gray smoke, dirt, and the smell of sulfur.

The 250-pound bomb had been electrically detonated in the midst of O'Bryan's point squad. As he lay on his back looking up, he saw the most peculiar sight. A single leg, covered in green, tumbling end over end at least fifty feet in the air. Everything seemed to move in slow motion. The leg rotated and turned for what seemed to be an eternity, as if it hung suspended in the universe and all else moved around it.

The explosion had temporarily deafened him to the moans of twenty marines. They lay spread below him like so many randomly discarded toy soldiers in a child's room. O'Bryan remained transfixed, his vision tunneled on the leg while its image burned into the deepest recess of his mind.

Nguyen was ecstatic. He had timed the explosion perfectly to create the most damage. He watched now from the hillside, in awe of the explosion, as parts of the Americans were scattered across the valley floor.

When the lead American had stopped Nguyen had held his breath. He knew the bomb and the wire leading from it could not possibly be seen, even though the man stopped and appeared to be looking directly at it. But then he had continued forward to within ten meters of the bomb. Just a little further, just a little further Nguyen had thought. Then he had pressed the contact switch together. His ears still rang from the explosion.

Suddenly there was rifle fire to Nguyen's left. He had told the team there was to be no firing, and he knew without looking it was Lot. Lot was exposing them all. He would kill Lot for this if the Americans did not. Two bullets cracked over his head and he saw a lone figure standing atop a small rise 200 meters away.

O'Bryan sprang to his feet. He saw a small figure raise out of the bush, on the hillside to his right front and fire at dazed marines in the valley. He was outraged. For a moment his vision blurred to reddish hues. He wiped tears from his eyes, raised his rifle and fired at the figure on the hillside.

He was not aware that he was running towards the hillside as he fired. He shouted, "Motherfuckers!" and changed magazines. He saw two more figures now.

Nothing in the world mattered to him, not bullets, not bombs, not even himself. He would kill them now, he could see them. He now ran at full speed to close the distance between them. He wanted to see their faces when they died.

Now there was firing behind him and he became aware of others following him. He saw another enemy figure running on the hillside. He dropped to one knee, fired another magazine, dropped the empty clip and replaced it.

O'Bryan had closed to the base of the hill, but had no idea how he got there. His lungs ached and his legs tingled.

He pulled a baseball shaped M33 hand grenade from an oversized pocket, pulled the pin and heaved it in his best outfielders form, forty meters up the hill. The grenade exploded exactly where he had last seen the figures running.

"Where they at, man?"

O'Bryan turned and saw Highfield and four other members of second squad on the ground behind him.

"You see where I threw the grenade?"

"Yeah."

"That's the last place I saw them."

Highfield came up to one knee holding the M6o machine gun by a bipod leg, with the gun slung waist high from over his shoulder. He fired short bursts into the gray cloud of the grenade explosion. The other squad members joined in and O'Bryan threw another grenade. There was no return fire.

"Cease fire!"

O'Bryan turned and saw Cpl. Johnson from second squad.

"They were right up there," O'Bryan pointed.

"They probably took off." Johnson looked around him.

"Hightower, you, Grenier and Orr stay here as a base of fire. O'Bryan, the rest of us will follow you. Work your way up to the right and above where you saw them. Then we'll come across and envelop their position."

It took them five minutes to cautiously move into position. When they arrived where Nguyen and his men had been, they found four empty spider trap holes in the ground. O'Bryan noted with satisfaction, there was a pool of blood soaking into the ground next to one of the holes. On the ground further up the hill they found the wire and electrical contact switch.

O'Bryan and Johnson looked down to the valley and surveyed the dark crater where O'Bryan's squad had stood.

Two medevac helicopters appeared overhead. A Huey

gunship made a pass down the valley attempting to draw fire. A green smoke grenade popped on the valley floor. O'Bryan sat down, suddenly exhausted. He put his face in his hands.

Johnson tried to raise Lt. Henderson on the radio. There was ominous silence, then Capt. Hudson came on. "Hold your positions until the choppers clear the area. You're in good shape to spot any hostile fire."

Johnson turned to his squad. "Keep your eyes peeled. Skipper wants us to stay up here until the medevacs leave."

They waited while the helicopters swooped in and picked up the wounded, then they retraced their route to the valley floor.

The remnants of Third Platoon searched for the body parts of O'Bryan's squad. The parts were collected and placed in green body bags. The mangled twisted parts of rifles and other gear were stacked next to them.

O'Bryan sat near the L.Z. area. He could not walk another step. He knew it had been Williams leg he had seen in the air. He did not know why he knew it. It was enough to know that it was. He sat there watching the mountainside. A hollow numbness spread over him from the center of his stomach. Soon he could feel nothing.

Nguyen and Dat Trung had covered four kilometers from the ambush site. They carefully picked their way along the jungle mountainsides and waited at a rendezvous point. Lt. Nguyen had decided that they would wait until morning for Trung Ly and Lot. For the first kilometer or so, he thought they were trailing behind him. He had stopped and waited several times, but there was no sign of them.

Dat Trung said that he thought Lot had been shot and last saw Ly helping him along the hillside.

"It serves him right," Nguyen had replied. "He could have cost all of us our lives, not to mention endangering the mission."

He felt uneasy waiting at the rendezvous point. If Lot and Ly were captured, Lot would surely tell the Americans where he and Dat Trung were waiting. He purposely sat up not at the designated spot, but on a nearby mountainside overlooking the meeting point. They had enough food for two more days, then they would return to the relative safety of the patrol base in Laos.

Nguyen sat with his back against a tree trunk chewing a piece of dried fish. *The marines are noisy and clumsy in the jungle, but I have to give them their due. They do not lack courage. I could have easily shot the man who charged us, but any delay might have been fatal.* He took a small sip of water from his canteen. *They are brave, but foolish.*

He would remember this lesson. This foolishness made them unpredictable and a more dangerous foe. He would include that in his briefing to his Regimental Commander.

The Commander would be waiting for his information, along with the intelligence from the team which had gone to survey the base a Long Vei. He knew the next time he met the marines, the odds would be in his favor.

*　　*　　*

The change in O'Bryan began soon after he returned to the base. He helped carry the green rubber body bags from the helicopter pad to a tin building, which served as graves registration at Khe Sanh. He wondered which one held the leg. The hollow numbness that had started at his center now enclosed him in a void.

The Captain had him write a contact report on the enemy soldiers he had charged after the bomb blast. No one else had seen them. He was also asked to collect all the squad's personal effects and bring them to the Company Command Post.

That night he had a bunker all to himself. He was the Second Squad until replacements arrived. He fell into an exhausted sleep. It was the first night he had the dream. He awakened in the middle of the night with the leg tumbling through his mind. He stayed awake until he felt the void again and knew it was safe to sleep.

He spoke only when spoken to. The new men said he was unfriendly. The older hands in the platoon said he was spooky. He ate by himself and constantly scanned the mountains around Khe Sanh. At every opportunity he studied a topographical map of the surrounding hills and valleys. At night he began to volunteer for listening posts outside the wire. No one argued with him.

One morning he returned from a listening post 100 meters from the south end of the airstrip wire. He had a strange look on his face. It was described by those who saw him as sort of a smile. In his right hand he held two khaki caps with distinctive red stars on the front. He told the new platoon commander, Lt. Masters, that he had found the caps on the way back to the perimeter.

He tossed them at two of the new squad members in

the bunker. "Souvenirs," he said, and walked away. They noticed blood on the caps was not yet dry.

No one knew what he did or where he went when he was out there at night. It became a heated topic of discussion among the grunts. But no one asked O'Bryan and he said nothing. He just sat and watched the hills.

It was only a matter of time until the rumors filtered back to Lt. Masters. Masters did not know exactly how to approach O'Bryan, and decided that he would confer with the Company Gunnery Sergeant. Gunny Timmons was part of the old breed and like SSgt. Alvarez had the automatic respect of every man in B Company.

Two nights later O'Bryan again volunteered for a listening post. He sat on the sandbagged roof of his bunker with his face blackened waiting for darkness. He looked up and saw Gunnery Sergeant Timmons walking towards him. The gunny sat down on the bunker roof next to him and looked out towards the perimeter.

"How's it goin', O'Bryan?"

"Can't complain, Gunny."

"You been through some rough times lately."

"Yeah."

"You know, people get real superstitious in combat. Heard of a guy in the 9th Marines had a brownie that his wife sent him from home. He never ate it, just carried it around in aluminum foil. Said it was his good luck piece. One day some joker in his squad got it and ate it. The guy found out it was missing and went ape. Next day he caught a sniper round in the throat. Guy who ate the brownie thought sure as hell he had killed his buddy. Some guys in the Company are startin' to get that way about you O'Bryan. Some of 'em think you're good luck, some of them think you're a jinx."

"Gunny, I'm at the point where I really don't give a shit what those guys think."

The gunny slowly pulled a pack of cigarettes from his pocket and lit one up. He inhaled deeply and sat quietly for a moment, then continued. "Scuttlebutt goin' around that you been leavin' your listening post at night and goin' on one-man patrols out there."

O'Bryan sat motionless on the bunker roof. He did not respond.

"Of course that's just rumors. If I could prove you did that I'd court martial your ass in a second."

"Do what you think is right Gunny."

"I heard you had a run-in with a tiger on 881 one night. You know a tiger is the baddest thing in the jungle out there at night. If that cat hadn't been starved crazy and half sick, he would never been out there huntin' by himself at night. Even they like to hunt in pairs. I hear First Platoon found him about 300 meters out. Said he had two or three bullet wounds. Of course a big cat just kills to eat or protect his own. He makes a clean kill."

"What's the difference, a kill is a kill Gunny."

"There's a difference, O'Bryan. The wrong kind comes back to you at night. Take my word for it. I been doin' this a lot longer than you have. Hell, Alvarez, the lieutenant, them guys in your squad, they were all my friends too."

O'Bryan turned his head slowly and looked at Timmons's dark, creased face. His voice was flat. "I got one for Alvarez, and one for the lieutenant. Tonight I'll get one for Williams."

"No you won't. I got your extension orders ready. You leave tomorrow morning on the resupply plane. Where do you want to take your leave?"

"I'm not ready yet, Gunny."

"You need a break kid, and I'm givin' it to you. You leave in the morning and that's it. Now where you goin'?"

O'Bryan thought for a moment. "I got a letter from Williams's sister the other day. I sort of want to visit his family. I figure it's the least I can do."

"OK, I'll make out the leave orders tonight, Continental United States. Come by the Company C.P. at 0800. I'll have the travel orders ready."

The gunny stood up to go and cast a long shadow over the bunker as darkness crept across the plateau. "Think about it, Son. Some of us have tigers that eat from the inside out. You're a marine. We hunt in groups and we make clean kills."

O'Bryan sat on the bunker and watched the darkness spread from the surrounding mountains. He knew that Gunny Timmons was right. Something inside him was broken. He felt no fear, and this served him well. The empty numbness had become his most deadly weapon. But the price was too high. It must be, he thought, what people felt when they lost their souls.

A mosquito bit him on the left arm. He swatted it and blood smeared down his arm from the engorged insect. He had killed the two North Vietnamese with the same detachment as he had the mosquito. He remembered the warmth of the blood when he cut their throats while they slept. He had found the little base camp while on a patrol with the rest of the platoon about 600 meters out. It was deserted but he thought they might return there, so he marked it on his map. They really weren't that good in the night when they didn't expect you. Very sloppy of them, he thought. One of them should have been awake. Of course who would have thought one man would come crawling along in the night. He still owed them for Williams, and the gunny forcing him to go on leave didn't change that. Patience was something new he had learned in the night. There would be other times. He shook his head and jumped down from the bunker roof to the trench line.

Chapter Four

Today, a letter had come from Susan Williams. He had not yet opened it. He ducked inside the bunker and pulled down the poncho which covered the entrance. He lit a candle, sat it on an empty ammunition crate, and picked up the letter from his dead friend's sister. He opened the letter and looked at the handwriting. It was very neat script, nearly straight up and down.

Dear John,

I feel I must write this letter to you. Doug's funeral was held yesterday. His last letter to me arrived three days before we were notified of his death. I was not even sure if you were alive, but I checked with the Red Cross and they say you are. Doug mentioned you in nearly every letter. I know you were very close friends and the loss must also be devastating to you. I expect you were there when he died and I hope you weren't injured. I have many questions about his death which are still unanswered.

Doug's last letter went on and on about finding you a pen pal and what a great time you guys were going to have when you returned. I still can't believe he's gone. As Doug may have told you, I think this whole thing is insane and idiotic. It must stop! I know you may not agree, but that's the way I feel.

You and Doug had such a short time left over there.

I hope you will be coming home safe soon. In the meantime, please write me. I promise to answer every letter. When you come back home, you must stop in L.A. and visit me and my parents. They would love to meet you. My address is 1115 Rollingwood Court, Apt. 215. My phone is 214-962-1852.

Your Friend,
Susan Williams

O'Bryan stared at the letter in the flickering light. He knew it was useless to reply. He was leaving in the morning and in all probability would arrive in Los Angles before the letter. He decided that he would call her when he got there. But what would he say to her?

They did have some things in common. She wanted answers. How did her brother die? O'Bryan also wanted answers. Why did Doug die, and why was he still alive? He could never tell her the truth. That her brother was blown into a hundred chunks of meat. That his disembodied leg haunted his dreams. That he was alive because a pissy little leech bit him on the leg.

Maybe he was alive because God has a lousy sense of humor. He began to laugh aloud. He suddenly realized that it was the first time since the ambush that he had laughed or cried.

He folded the letter, placed it in his shirt pocket and blew out the candle. He lay back on his air mattress with his hands behind his head. He would visit Doug's family and tell them how it happened. Tears spilled down his cheeks and a merciful dead sleep overcame him.

The next morning he was up at 6 a.m., feeling rested

and refreshed after an uninterrupted night. He walked from his bunker to the trench line. The other men in the platoon were asleep, trying to capture a few more precious minutes of rest after standing night watches.

He pulled the liner from his helmet, filled it with water, then washed and shaved. He ate a leisurely breakfast of beans and weenies and opened a can of C-ration pears, which he had been saving for a special occasion. By 9 a.m. he had collected his orders from Gunny Timmons and turned in his rifle and ammunition to the Battalion Armorer. He said his goodbyes to his squad. Even though he did not know the new men very well, he was entrusted with a couple of phone messages to deliver when he reached the United States.

By 10 a.m. the fog had burned off around the steel-matted runway. A C-123 wearing its brown and green war paint, lumbered down and landed. A forklift quickly attended to the unloading of the plane. O'Bryan boarded the empty plane, strapped himself in a jump seat, and within thirty minutes landed at the huge Da Nang air base.

Twenty-four hours later he was in Okinawa at a Marine transit barracks. His old clothing was burned, and he was issued a new set of uniforms, along with a regulation hair cut. He was prodded and poked by doctors and any item he had from Vietnam was seized. After being completely sanitized of the war he passed a formal inspection by a young lieutenant and was booked on a flight to CONUS (Continental United States).

Seventy-eight hours after leaving the trenchline at Khe Sanh, he boarded a contracted T.W.A. 747, en route from Okinawa to Los Angles. The men boarded the plane in silent awe. It was a holy moment. No one spoke for fear they might jinx themselves or awaken from this dream.

O'Bryan made certain that he was one of the first to board the plane. He had once read that passengers seated near the tail section of an airliner had the best chance of surviving a crash. Let the officers have the first class section, he thought, I won't have to pull my head from the copilot's ass if we ditch over the ocean.

He picked a seat in the last row next to the plane's galley. The two seats next to him were reserved for the flight crew. The mood of the men on the plane had lifted. They were now like children waiting to open packages on Christmas morning.

These were the ones who made it, he thought. O'Bryan smiled and looked around at his fellow survivors. Every man sat mesmerized as a vision of American beauty explained emergency procedures.

She had short red hair and striking green eyes. Each man on the plane traced the outline of her body with his eyes. O'Bryan figured most of the grunts on the plane would kill each other off in case of a crash, trying to get her into a raft.

Finally the plane taxied and lifted off the runway. As the plane took off, soldiers, a few sailors, and marines stood in the aisle and began to cheer and yell. "Back to the world, baby!" "We made it!" "Alright!"

All three stewardesses attempted to maintain order and keep their exuberant passengers seated. It was no use. They were grabbed, fondled, and kissed until they finally retreated to the rear of the plane, directly behind where O'Bryan was seated.

The three women stood there with bemused smiles and smeared lipstick, adjusting their clothing.

O'Bryan remained seated. It was not his celebration. He was not finished with the war. At the direction of some officers in first class, the celebrants returned to their seats and strapped themselves down. Order was restored.

He sunk into the high-backed passenger seat and closed his eyes. The rumble of the jet engines sent a faint vibration through the seat and up his spine. The strong smell of fresh coffee being brewed by the stewardesses behind him mingled with the smell of their perfume and created a sweet stimulant in the air.

He felt relaxed for the first time in months. It was safe up here, suspended at 30,000 feet. He slowly opened his eyes and glanced out the small oval window next to him.

He watched the clouds and the blue sea below. How peculiar he felt. He was coming back in thirty days. He thought of the dead left behind. Far below he knew that life opened and closed, but somehow now he could not be touched by it.

"Do you want coffee?"

He looked up into the sparkling blue eyes of a blond stewardess. Her hair was mussed from the celebration/molestation.

"Yes, ma'am."

"Cream and sugar?"

"Yes, ma'am."

She handed him the cup and moved on.

He sipped the coffee and glanced up to see the no smoking, fasten seat belt signs were now off.

A young soldier in the middle of the cabin retrieved a guitar from an overhead storage compartment. He tuned the guitar for a moment then began a song. It wasn't Eric Burdon, but O'Bryan recognized the song instantly. It was the universal theme song of all grunts. Men began to join in the chorus.

"We gotta get out of this place."

"If it's the last thing we ever do."

"We gotta get out of this place."

"Girl there's a better life for me and you."

O'Bryan did not sing. Instead, he thought about what he would do when he arrived. It would be Christmas time when he landed in the world.

A long suppressed shadow crept across his mind. A seven-year-old boy in pajamas. Christmas morning. Looking at the presents under the tree. A nude woman in a bathtub. Pools of blood around her arms. Momma! He pushed his mother's suicide back into its mental cave.

He would not return to Oklahoma. There was nothing there for him. He would try to call his little sister; she was living with an Aunt. He would not try to find his father. There was no sense in opening old wounds. *If anyone should look for anyone, he should look for me. All he had to do was contact the Red Cross. Susan Williams found me easily enough.* But he knew his father would not.

He decided he would stay in California. Maybe go to the beach, take in some movies, eat good. He would have to rent a car, go see the Williams family and then play it by ear.

He had plenty of money saved, and decided that wherever he went, whatever he did, he would have a good time. *I might not make the next trip back.*

He sat the empty coffee cup on the fold-up tray in front of him. The excitement of the flight had begun to wear off. The soldier with the guitar softly strummed Simon and Garfunkels's "The Sounds of Silence." O'Bryan leaned his head against the cabin bulkhead and dozed off.

Lt. Nguyen stood back from the edge of the 600-meter sheer cliff. He held up his binoculars and looked towards the Marine base at Khe Sanh. Though he was standing just inside the Laotian border, the base was well within the range of his 122mm rockets. He could see black smoke rising from the marines' trash fires.

He had been directed to guide and help set up a battery of these rockets along the face of the cliffs. Men would be lowered by rope down the side of the cliff, to take advantage of the natural shelter afforded by the caves in the rock walls. He was accompanied by a small group of engineers and builders who would help set the rockets into firing position.

Dat Trung stood next to him and read an azimuth from his compass to the base. The distance to the target had already been measured down to the meter.

"These will be excellent positions, Lieutenant. Once the rocket batteries are established in the caves, only a direct hit from an American plane will knock them out."

"We will pray that the low clouds and fog keep the planes away. Tell the engineers to keep noise to a minimum. Sound travels in these mountains. We don't want them to know we are here until we're ready."

Dat started to walk off and deliver this message to the engineer officer, then stopped and turned towards his lieutenant.

"Did you speak to the Guards Colonel this morning?"
"Yes."

"Any news of Trung Ly or Lot?"

"No, they are still missing."

"Did you hear about the two men found with their throats cut?"

"Yes probably some of Lot's Montagnard cousins."

"Do you think that's what happened to them?"

"I don't know. If he is alive, Trung Ly will try to make it back to us. Who can say about Lot. He is without any sense of duty. He will fight for whoever feeds him."

"How long do we have to complete these positions?"

"Not long."

"The attack is scheduled to begin in January. It will be coordinated with other strikes. We will annihilate the Americans on the hills, overrun the base, then drive along highway 9 and join forces with units at Quang Tri and Hue. The people will rise up all over the south and overthrow the puppet government. There will be so many Americans killed that their people will lose heart and demand action to end the war."

"Do you think the war will soon be over?"

"Yes, soon. Thousands of trucks are on the way. Two artillery units and two armored units, over 30,000 men. Dat, did you know that we are with the same Guards unit who won at Dien Bien Phu?"

"No."

"Yes, the Colonel told me. The 304th Division, the Hanoi Guards. It is destiny. This will be the Americans' Dien Bien Phu."

O'Bryan felt a hand on the back of his head.

Instinctively his hand shot up and grabbed his enemy by the throat. The stewardess dropped the small white pillow and screamed as he sat bolt upright in his seat.

He realized immediately what he had done and let go of the woman's throat. It was the blond with the wide blue eyes who had served him coffee.

Several drowsy heads turned to see what was happening and another stewardess hurried to the back of the plane. O'Bryan's face flushed.

"I'm sorry, miss, I am really sorry."

The stewardess had nearly recovered and stood holding a hand to her throat. "It's OK, I'm alright. I was afraid your neck would get sore."

She bent down and picked up the pillow.

"Here, put this behind your head."

"Thank you. Are you sure you're OK?"

She was blushing now.

"I'm fine, just fine."

She turned and walked back to the galley. O'Bryan could hear her talking in whispers to another stewardess. He slumped down in his seat and tried to become invisible.

"Here, Marine."

He looked up and found it was the same blond stewardess offering him a clear plastic cup of Coke.

"Thank you."

She handed him the cup and then sat in the seat next to him and sipped from her own cup. She turned and looked at him.

"Drink up, we could both use it."

He took a big drink from the cup and found it was half coke and half bourbon. He wrinkled his nose in surprise and sat up.

She smiled and leaned towards him.

"It's against the rules you know, to serve liquor on any of these military flights. But we keep some for emergencies, and I think you and I have had one."

"I'm really embarrassed, miss."

"Don't be, and call me Jane, Jane Culbert."

O'Bryan quickly extended his hand.

"O'Bryan, John O'Bryan. I didn't bruise you or anything?"

She smiled, exposing two perfect dimples at the corners of her mouth and a blinding set of white teeth.

"No John, as a matter of fact, my neck is about the only place on my body where I'm not bruised."

O'Bryan laughed and felt the warmth of the bourbon in his stomach. He felt a little loose and bold.

"Those guys did get a little out of hand when we took off. But some of them haven't seen a woman in a long time, much less someone as pretty as you are."

"I think there is a bit of the blarney in you, Mr. O'Bryan. Where are you from?"

"Oklahoma."

"Oklahoma, ever play football?"

"No, too skinny."

"How long were you in Vietnam?"

"Twelve months."

"Was it rough over there?"

"It could get that way sometimes."

She paused for a moment and drained the rest of the drink. "You got a girl back home?"

"Not anymore."

"Sorry," she said placing a hand on his forearm.

"Don't worry, a nice-looking kid like you, it won't take

long to find another one."

O'Bryan felt his face flushing again. She stood up. "Well I better get back there and start the meals. I don't want any of these guys to get hungry."

O'Bryan drained the plastic glass and handed it to her. She smiled one of those blinding smiles again.

"Talk to you later."

In thirty minutes the meals were served. O'Bryan ate the small portion of beef and noodles and drank a coke. The tray was taken by the red-headed stewardess, and he lit up a cigarette.

Jane came back with another drink.

"Here you go."

He leaned for the glass and she gave him a kiss on the cheek.

"In case no one else tells you, welcome home."

Then she turned and walked back to the galley.

O'Bryan sat back with the drink. A warm glow surrounded him. He finished the drink, then stubbed the cigarette out and sat the empty cup on the seat next to him.

Civilization, he thought, *this is what we are fighting for.* Then the food and drinks overcame him.

Jane the stewardess returned and spread a blanket over him, staying cautiously out of reach.

The next thing he heard was the voice of the captain of the plane.

"We are now descending to make our approach to Los Angeles International Airport. The local time is 5:37 p.m. On behalf of myself and the crew we would like to thank you for flying T.W.A."

In thirty minutes he was on the ground inside the mammoth terminal. The Christmas rush seemed to have already started. It was wall-to-wall people. There were servicemen everywhere he turned. He found a television terminal and looked for the baggage claim area where his seabag would arrive. He took a moving sidewalk to the baggage area and watched the people shove each other and hurry past.

He stood leaning against a giant white pillar and waited for the conveyor belt to produce his bag. A feeling of panic came over him as he realized he was completely alone.

CHAPTER FIVE

O'Bryan waited for forty-five minutes at the car rental counter. The rental area had two counter girls working, when there should have been five. The area was full of men in suits carrying briefcases and overcoats.

He dragged his bulky green seabag behind him and took his place in line. He looked around and noticed that he seemed to be the only person in this area in uniform. The line inched forward. It took him another forty-five minutes to reach the front of the counter.

A heavyset girl wearing a tight-fitting blue blazer with bleach blond hair stood facing him. She reached under the counter, came up with some forms and slapped them down on the counter in front of him.

"I'll need a valid driver's license, military I.D., and your travel orders."

O'Bryan began to dig in his pockets for his I.D. and orders. He placed them on the counter along with his state driver's license. The plump blond bent over and carefully examined the three documents.

"This license has been expired for over a year," she stated without looking up.

"I know that, but as long as I am in the military I don't have to renew it."

"I'll need a $200 cash deposit or a credit card, if you want a car. You don't have a credit card do you?"

"No, Ma'am, but I have $200."

O'Bryan filled out the forms she shoved at him. He noticed that she smiled and said "No, sir," and "yes, sir," to the civilian businessmen, but seemed to look through him.

"I am finished filling these out, miss."

"Alright, I'll be with you in a minute."

She waited on several more people and then walked back to him from the far end of the counter.

He was accustomed to waiting in lines and flying standby status. It seemed to him that the uniform marked him as a second class citizen. However, now he was paying the same rate everyone else was paying and he found the girl's rudeness hard to tolerate.

She handed him a set of keys with a number on them. "It's number 52, a blue Ford. Make sure the tank is full when you return it."

He paid her, took his copy of the rental agreement and left. The blue Ford was nearly the last car in the agency parking lot. He got in the car and sat for a moment, wondering where he should go.

He decided to drive towards downtown Los Angeles and see if he could find a nice hotel. He had only been to L.A. once before and that had been on a bus. He decided he should get a map when he found a place to stay.

The traffic around the airport was thick with holiday commuters. He again found himself waiting in a long line of cars trying to enter the freeway.

He sat in the car with the windows down and smoked a cigarette. He leaned sideways and looked up at the sky. It was a patented southern California day. The smog had lifted, and the air had a fresh cool ocean smell. The sun was low on the horizon and would soon dip into the sea west of him.

He thought he might go out tonight and order the thickest steak at the most expensive restaurant he could find. He had saved $4000 while he was in Vietnam and he intended to live well for the next thirty days.

He looked down at his hands and smiled. If it were not for the uniform, he could nearly believe the war was a distant nightmare and he had just awakened. As he looked around at the cars full of happy well fed people, he found it difficult to believe there was a war. Except for him, there was no sign of it anywhere.

He noticed an unusual smell in the air and saw white steam rising from the hood of the Ford. The red light that indicates overheating began to blink on the instrument display. He made a fist.

"Shit!" he yelled, and pounded the dash board.

He pulled out of the line of cars leading to the on ramp and parked on the shoulder. He flipped on the emergency blinkers and got out to raise the hood.

He stared down helplessly and looked at steam rolling out from under the radiator.

He retrieved his seabag from the back seat of the car and began the long walk back to the airport. A fine mist of sweat began to form on him and his uniform shirt stuck to his back in dark blots. The seabag strap dug into his shoulder. He was amazed at the collection of trash along the roadway and kicked at food wrappers and tin cans while he silently cursed the rental agency, the Marine Corps, and the Ford Motor Company.

Thirty minutes later he arrived back at the rental counter exhausted. The crowd had thinned out some and he approached the same girl who had rented him the car.

"Miss, I rented a car from you and it broke down before I could get on the freeway, overheated."

She looked up at him.

"As soon as I finish waiting on these gentlemen I'll give you a replacement form to fill out. You also need to get in line."

O'Bryan's voice grew louder and he felt blood rushing to his head.

"There are no signs saying where to stand."

He had her full attention now.

"Can't you see everyone else standing over here?" She pointed to the men standing opposite her at the counter. Now all the customers standing around began to watch the small confrontation.

O'Bryan paused, put down his bag and exhaled a little air. "Listen, miss, I just want my money back, here's the keys for number 52 and my receipt."

She ignored the paper and keys.

"I'm sorry, we can not refund cash, it's in the contract. We can give you another car if you get back in line."

O'Bryan's voice rose ten decibels.

"I don't want another car from you, I want my money back." She looked at him for a moment, her pale face slightly flushed.

"Please do not yell at me."

A man wearing an identical blue blazer with some sort of logo on the breast pocket, emerged from a door behind the counter. The loud voices must have carried into his office. He walked to the opposite side of the counter, where O'Bryan stood.

"I'm the manager here, what seems to be the problem?"

O'Bryan looked at the man who appeared to be around thirty, six feet tall, with a slight paunch. After a short pause he took a breath, and repeated his story.

"I rented a car from you and it broke down. Now I would like my money back."

He stopped, then added, "It's very simple."

The blond broke in.

"I told him we don't refund cash."

The manager nodded.

"I heard."

The manager then placed both hands palms down on the counter and leaned forward.

"Listen, kid, I'll give you another car and you can be on your way."

O'Bryan didn't respond.

The manager screwed up his mouth and gave him a look of contempt and exasperation.

"Look, kid, it's not my problem if you can't read, you signed the agreement."

O'Bryan and the manager stood for a moment longer, their faces separated by only a few inches. All eyes in the room were focused on them.

The manager played to the small crowd by throwing up his arms in melodramatic style.

"Where did you leave the car?"

O'Bryan responded in a soft low voice.

"About a mile from here by the northbound on ramp."

"OK kid, get to the end of the line or get out."

"Could I see my original rental contract?"

"Sure," the manager said rolling his eyes.

The girl shuffled through a stack of papers, found the form and gave it to her boss. He in turn handed it ceremoniously to O'Bryan.

O'Bryan looked at the paper and thought about what he had done to earn that $200. It was blood money.

If anyone from his squad had been present they would have backed away. They would have recognized the half bent smile on his face. O'Bryan continued in the same soft low voice.

"OK, you keep my money, but here's something to go with it."

It wasn't a great punch, his weight was not behind it. However, it was delivered with cobra-like quickness. It caught the manager flat footed and stationary, and landed square on the side of his face, spinning him halfway around.

The plump blond screamed and everyone else stood frozen.

O'Bryan deliberately shouldered his bag, turned and walked out the automatic door exit.

He could hear onlookers yelling at him, but had a curious feeling of detachment, as if he was also a spectator here.

He knew he had lost control and made an ass of himself. It was not the manager who enraged him. He just happened to be in the wrong place. It was nothing personal.

Inside the terminal at the rental agency, the manager sat on the floor holding his head. Someone shouted.

"Call the police, I'll be a witness, that guy's crazy."

The blond knelt down next to her boss.

Looking down she said, "He's dangerous, he ought to be locked up."

O'Bryan continued to walk down the broad terminal sidewalk. He did not know or care where he was headed. He muttered to himself as he walked.

"This is great, no car now. The police are coming to

find me and I'm dragging this damn bag around like an anchor."

He spotted a taxi parked next to the curb fifty feet ahead. He walked quickly to the back door of the cab, opened it and threw in his bag.

"Take me to the best hotel in downtown L.A."

"That's a long ride buddy, it'll cost ya."

"No problem."

"How about the Biltmore?"

"Sounds good to me," said O'Bryan as he slouched down in the well worn back seat.

The cab driver shrugged his shoulders started the meter and drove off.

The taxi driver claimed to be a World War II Marine veteran. He talked through the Guadalcanal campaign and was well into the Iwo Jima landing when they arrived at the Biltmore hotel on South Grand.

"You see, son, that was war, and you knew what was right and wrong. Hell, you don't know in this thing who's worse, the ones you're fightin' for or the ones you're fightin' against."

O'Bryan nodded patiently and then paid his fare.

It was the biggest hotel O'Bryan had ever seen. A doorman stepped out from behind two wide automatic doors and took his bag.

O'Bryan followed the man with his bag to a large oak registration counter. The hotel lobby had a huge cut glass chandelier suspended from a cathedral-like ceiling. Dark ornate woodwork outlined the doorways and walls. It was old and O'Bryan thought it must have been very elegant at one time. Now, chipped paint and worn carpet showed it had been neglected in recent years.

He checked in and paid for three days in advance. A bell boy about his age carried his seabag to the elevator and then to his room on the tenth floor.

The room was as old-fashioned as the lobby. A four poster double bed was covered by a royal blue bedspread and sat on a neutral tan carpet.

The bell boy opened matching blue drapes and exposed large casement windows with a view of the roof of the building next door. O'Bryan offered him a tip, but the young bellhop raised his hand in refusal. He pointed to the ribbons on O'Bryan's shirt.

"You been in Vietnam?"

O'Bryan nodded yes and the boy continued.

"I thought I might have to go, but I was enrolled in a Junior College, you know, got a student deferment. Sometimes I wish I had gone. Some of my high school buddies did."

O'Bryan interrupted, "Say, where's the place to go here in L.A., I'm not from around here."

The boy answered immediately.

"Same place as always, the Strips what's happening at night. Everyone is home from school on Christmas break. But I wouldn't wear that uniform, they aren't real popular right now. I mean if you want to meet some girls or something."

O'Bryan smiled, "Sure, thanks for the advice."

The boy started for the door.

"Hey, don't think about it, have a good time."

"I'll try, thanks."

The boy closed the door and O'Bryan stood in the middle of the room. He felt as out of place as his seabag looked in the big walk-in closet.

He sat on the edge of the bed and looked across the room into a bathroom with a large vanity done in black marble and blue tile. The whole place looked very luxurious to him. He fell back on the bed slowly.

He lay there for a moment and decided he should call his sister. He pulled a small black notebook from his breast pocket and found her number. He placed the call through the hotel operator and fought the urge to hang up as the phone rang at the other end.

"Hello?"

"Jennifer, it's me, Johnny."

"Johnny! where are you?"

"In Los Angeles."

"When did you get back from Vietnam?"

"Today, I just got in and checked into a hotel."

"When are you coming home?"

"You mean Oklahoma?"

"I mean here, Oklahoma City."

"I wasn't planning on coming there."

"Why not?"

"I just decided to hang around out here."

"That's ridiculous, it's Christmas time, Aunt Joan and Uncle Fred want to see you, and I won't forgive you if you don't come home for Christmas."

"Come on Jennifer, give me a little slack."

"Johnny, Dad's in town."

"Is he sober?"

There was a long pause on the other end.

"I take that to be a no. You remember what happened the last time I saw him?"

The mental image of O'Bryan's father, drunk and raising a black leather belt to hit Jennifer flashed in his mind.

O'Bryan had hit him harder than he had hit anyone in his life. He was afraid he had killed him, but he was only passed out. He and Jennifer had carried him to his bedroom and dumped him on the bed. O'Bryan had left the next morning on a bus for boot camp, while his father still lay snoring in bed.

"Johnny, that was a long time ago, and he was drunk. When he came to, he didn't remember what had happened. He felt terrible."

"Has he straightened out any?"

"He tries, Johnny, he really tries, but he just can't seem to make it."

"Jen, I just don't think it would be a good idea for me to see him again."

"Well, at least come back and see us. What about Sherri?"

"That's all history now."

"You broke up?"

"Afraid so. How's high school?"

"Boring, but we're on Christmas break next week. I'm playing basketball, we have a game tomorrow."

"You on offense or defense?"

"I'm forward. I got a 14-point a game average."

"Got a boyfriend?"

"I don't have time for boys right now. Between schoolwork and playing ball, I'm pretty busy."

"Listen, Jen, I am gonna go now. Don't want to run up too big a bill. I'll call again when I work out what I'm gonna do for sure."

"At least think about coming home to see us. You don't have to see Dad."

"I'll think about it, and you think about what you want for Christmas. Good luck in your game."

"Bye."

"Bye, Jen."

He sat the phone back on the receiver and took a deep breath. He lay back on the bed again and thought about his family.

After his mother's death, it had been just him, his dad, and Jen. His father had always had a drink or two, but the drinking became heavier until it grew to a compulsion completely out of control.

His father got very mean when he was drunk and would sometimes beat O'Bryan and his sister. O'Bryan had learned to hate his father's black leather belt. It left red welts on him and his sister.

When his father was sober, he would cry and say he was sorry he hit them, but he would get drunk and it would happen again. O'Bryan and his sister had learned to hide when he came home late at night. He would go room to room shouting for them until he passed out. Only then was it safe to come out. It was like living with a time bomb, always wondering when he would go off.

Soon his father lost his job and then it was worse. At times he would go on a bender and be gone for weeks. O'Bryan prayed at those times that he wouldn't return, but he always did. He grew to hate his father.

As soon as he was seventeen he joined the Marines. His father had been drunk the night he signed the permission form for him to enlist.

He had snarled at O'Bryan, "Get the hell out."

The house they lived in was scheduled to be repossessed and O'Bryan had arranged for his sister to live with an aunt and uncle. His father had disappeared and no one looked for him. By this time he had become one of the street people. The utilities had been cut off at the house and creditors hounded them constantly. After Sherri's letter there was just no reason to go back. There wasn't much left to call home.

He decided to phone Susan Williams and sat up again. The phone rang fifteen times without an answer. He sat the notebook next to the phone and hung up. Outside, darkness had fallen and a dull yellow haze hung over the city.

He lay back again and this time felt very tired. The next moment he was asleep.

He awakened the next day. Sunlight flooded the room through the west window. Someone was knocking on the door. He rubbed his eyes and staggered half asleep to the door. A short black woman with a housekeeping cart looked up at him.

"Room service, do you want the room cleaned?"

"No, thank you."

He closed the door and looked at his watch. It was five o'clock in the afternoon. He had slept nearly twenty-four hours. He tried to remember what day it was, but it eluded him.

"Sleeping my leave away," he said to himself.

He shed his uniform, shaved and took a long hot shower. He dressed in a new uniform shirt and broke out his dress green jacket and pants from the seabag. They were a little wrinkled, but he figured the wrinkles would fall out quickly.

His stomach growled.

"I know, I know," he said patting his belly.

He tried to call Susan Williams again but there was still no answer. He went to his seabag and dumped the contents on the floor. In the bottom, between two shirts, he pulled out a wad of cash. On the way out of the hotel he deposited all but $200 in the hotel safe.

He decided tonight he would go out on the town and see what he could find. He asked the desk clerk for a map and a bus schedule, then walked to the end of the block to the bus stop.

He waited through three buses before the one marked Sunset Blvd. over the windshield approached. He paid his fare and walked to a seat in the middle of the bus.

Excitement swelled within him. The neon lights sailed past as the bus went from one stop to another.

He noticed the traffic had become extremely heavy, almost bumper to bumper as they neared Hollywood Boulevard. Everywhere he looked he saw young people cruising up and down the street. This must be The Strip he thought.

The sidewalk crowd was a near mob scene in places. Young people moved shoulder to shoulder and stood in clustered groups. The bus reached a corner stop and he got out. As he stepped off the bus he saw a group of people playing instruments at the next corner.

When he was closer he saw they were street missionaries. A girl about his age handed him a leaflet.

"Have you met your personal savior, the Lord Jesus Christ?"

O'Bryan was thinking about that when she continued.

"If you haven't then you're not saved. After we finish playing here we are all going to a service. There will be free refreshments."

O'Bryan looked down at the leaflet, which said something about the end of the world.

"I'm sorry, but I am meeting some friends later."

"They are welcome too."

"Maybe some other time."

He walked for several blocks looking in the store windows and watching the people and cars. The noise and confusion completely engulfed him. A swell of humanity picked him up and lifted him from block to block.

His nose picked up the scent of hamburgers. It had been so very long since he had smelled that aroma. he tracked the scent to a storefront with a red neon sign that said "Deli."

He was about to enter the deli when a voice called.

"Hey, marine!"

O'Bryan turned and faced two young girls standing on the opposite side of the recessed entrance. One had brown hair and the other red.

The redhead was short and plump. The brunette was about five-foot ten and very slender. They both wore army surplus fatigues, with an assortment of patches and insignias. He thought neither one could be more than seventeen. The brunette took one step forward.

"Come here," she said and motioned with a curled index finger.

"What do you want?" he asked.

"How would you like to buy me a hamburger?" asked the tall one.

"Why should I?"

"Because me and my friend are dead broke."

O'Bryan looked at them for a moment. The brunette did look pale and thin. He was feeling generous and was a little dazed by the nighttime circus atmosphere.

"OK, come on and bring your friend."

They found a booth. The two girls both ordered a double cheeseburger and french fries. O'Bryan was famished. He ordered two cheeseburgers and fries with a malt.

The girls giggled to each other and wolfed down their food. O'Bryan found he was stuffed after eating only one cheeseburger. His stomach had shrunk to accommodate a C-ration diet. It would be some time before he could eat a heavy meal.

The girls eyed his plate.

"What's the matter, your food not any good?"

"No, it's just that I can't eat right now."

"Can we have the rest?"

"Be my guest." O'Bryan shoved his plate across the table.

"We don't usually eat like this," said the brunette between bites.

The redhead began to giggle. "It's just that we been smoking this really great shit."

"You know, marine, you're not a bad guy for a jarhead."

"Thanks."

"No really, I mean it. He's kind of cute, isn't he, Mitzi?"

This brought a mushed giggle from the redhead.

The brunette leaned across the table and extended her hand.

"My name is Mona and this is Mitzi."

O'Bryan shook her hand.

"How would you like to go to a party?"

O'Bryan did not reply.

"You'd be our guest. Just a little way to pay you back for the food."

"You don't owe me anything."

"I know, but it's not far from here.

"You got money for a taxi?" asked Mitzi.

"O'Bryan nodded yes.

The girls finished off the food, then waited for O'Bryan outside. By the time he had paid the ticket they had already stopped a taxi.

Mona stood by the open back door.

"Come on, marine."

O'Bryan stopped for a moment, then thought what the hell and jumped into the back seat. The driver had already been given the address. The taxi pulled away as soon as the door closed.

He sat silently in the back seat. The girls talked nonstop to each other. They commented on how pretty the lights were. This included stoplights, headlights, or anything else that shined.

The cab driver glanced occasionally in the rearview mirror when the girls got particularly loud.

Mona suddenly grew silent and glanced at O'Bryan as if she suddenly noticed him for the first time.

"What's your name?"

"John."

"Where you from?"

"Oklahoma."

Both girls broke into hysterical giggles.

"Jesus, Mitzi, a marine named John from Oklahoma."

O'Bryan decided that as soon as the cab arrived wherever the girls were going, he would drop them and go back to the hotel.

Mona pulled a pint of Jack Daniels from her fatigue jacket.

"You need to loosen up, honey, take a sip."

O'Bryan looked at the bottle for a moment then took a big gulp. It nearly made him gag and burned all the way down.

After ten more minutes and three more shots of whiskey, the cab pulled up in front of a duplex.

Mitzi sat up, "This is it."

O'Bryan had no idea where they were.

"Sorry, girls," he said as they got out.

"I'm a little tired. I think I'll take the cab back to the hotel."

"No way, John," whined Mona, "just pay the man and come on in."

O'Bryan shook his head and then paid the driver. The girls each grabbed one arm and squeezed him between them. They walked him to the front door of the duplex. He could hear music playing inside.

Mitzi reached forward and opened the door. Inside O'Bryan could see a living room, a dining kitchen area, and what appeared to be a doorway to a bedroom. He could not make out how many people were inside, because the only light was a small bulb over the kitchen sink.

A man's voice yelled, "Hey, Mitzi!"

"She drug in another god damned marine."

The whiskey had made O'Bryan light-headed, but this did not look like a party to him. There now seemed to be about eight forms in the room. The marijuana smell hung heavily in the air.

Aside from the two girls O'Bryan was with, it appeared to be an all-male gathering.

The girls steered him to an empty chair in the corner of the room. Mona sat on the arm of the chair still holding his hand. Mitzi walked towards two men seated on a ragged sofa. They were making a great show of smoking some pot.

O'Bryan sat in the chair with his back rigid. His eyes had grown accustomed to the dark and he could see he was surrounded by bikers.

Mitzi returned with a glass of beer.

"Here, drink this and relax. We're all friends here."

O'Bryan looked up at her. "Friends of what?"

Mitzi ignored the comment. Mona got up and walked to the kitchen. Mitzi took her place on the arm of the chair.

"I like you," she said. She began to squeeze his hand and kiss the nape of his neck. She whispered in his ear. "Have you got fifty dollars? How long has it been since you were with a woman?"

"A long time, but no thanks. Is there a phone here so I can call a taxi?"

"You don't like me?" asked Mitzi.

"It would be the best fifty bucks you ever spent."

O'Bryan turned in the chair. "Nothing personal."

"Will you at least loan me fifty bucks?"

O'Bryan began to feel funny. His face felt hot and his fingers tingled.

"Where's the phone?" he asked again.

"In the bedroom, come on, I'll show you."

O'Bryan had trouble standing, his legs felt like they were asleep. He followed Mitzi across the room to a doorway.

The wine bottle hit the back of his head about two steps into the room. *Dumb*, thought O'Bryan as the floor came up to meet him.

Nguyen moved cautiously across the valley floor of the Rao Quan River concealed by six-foot-high elephant grass. He was leading three new team members on a two-night journey around the American base at Khe Sanh and across the valley floor to the foot of hill 1015 overlooking the base. In addition to their own food, water, weapons and ammunition, they carried a 60mm mortar and 10 mortar rounds each. Another team with 75mm recoilless rifle would make the same trek and join them in a few days.

Nguyen's mission was to find a vantage point on the side of hill 1015 where he could assess damage done to the base by rocket and artillery fire. If possible they also were to fire mortar rounds at arriving aircraft in hopes of destroying one on the runway. He knew it would be a lucky shot but he couldn't wait for a chance to try. He silently signaled for the team to move out then paused for just moment and looked into the black moonless night. He wondered if he would ever see home again.

CHAPTER SIX

"Jesus George, you didn't need to hit him so hard. I put enough stuff in that beer to knock out two guys. He would have passed out in a minute."

"Shut up, Mitzi, you don't screw around with these guys. You got to do it hard and fast."

George, a heavyset biker with tattoos up and down both arms, bent down and rolled O'Bryan from his stomach to his back. A trickle of blood ran down the back of O'Bryan's head.

Mitzi leaned over and began to search the uniform pockets. She frowned a look of disgust at the blood dripping on the floor.

"You still shouldn't a hit him so hard. He was kinda cute."

George raised up and turned around to face two more bikers behind him.

"Mitzi, baby, you do good work. You hit a gold mine. Look at all the twenties."

Mitzi's frown changed quickly to a smile as George waved a handful of cash in the air.

"I can pick 'em, can't I, George?"

O'Bryan awakened to find himself in a narrow space between two buildings about thirty feet from a busy street.

The back of his head hurt and he felt the warm stickiness of blood in his matted hair. He gently touched other parts of his body checking for more damage.

Everything seemed to work.

He stood, felt dizzy and sick to his stomach. He tried to think back about what had happened. But he couldn't make his mind focus. Colors and noises seemed to filter through his head at lightning speed.

He fell back against the wall of a building, and his knees buckled under him as he squatted in the narrow alley. Tears of anger began to roll, and he shouted, "Son of a bitch." Then big, loud sobs echoed off the smooth concrete walls into the darkness. Time had no meaning. How long had he squatted there? His mind gradually began to slow down. He noticed his pockets were inside out. He shoved them back inside his pants and pushed himself up against the side of the wall.

He began to remember parts of the evening. He remembered the girls, the taxi ride, and the bikers, but it was all fragmented.

He walked out from the alley to a broad sidewalk and grasped a "No Parking" sign to steady himself. O'Bryan had no idea where he was.

A fuzzy plan began to take shape in his mind. He spoke to himself while holding on to the sign. "Need help."

O'Bryan reached into his left shirt pocket. It was unbuttoned, but the letter from Susan Williams and I.D. was still there. He did not try to take the letter out. He patted it and the act seemed to calm him.

Now he needed to find a telephone. He looked around for the first time. Cars whizzed by on the street a few feet away. Some people walked by and gave him peculiar looks, then walked a wide path around him.

He spotted another No Parking sign half a block away and decided his goal would be to make it there. About half the distance to the sign, the ground spun again and he fell hard on his left elbow.

He was struggling to get to his feet when a spotlight blinded him. Red and white flashing lights reflected off the store windows. He put a hand in front of his eyes and saw two huge black figures. The L.A.P.D. had found him.

"Too much fire water, marine?"

"Need help."

"I would say you do. Come on, partner. Let's get him up."

Two arms grabbed him on either side and lifted him from the sidewalk. They walked him to a police car and propped him against the side.

O'Bryan felt hands patting his arms and legs. One of the officers opened a car door and guided him into the back seat. The dome light came on and he saw that a black mesh barrier separated him from the front seat. The doors closed and the light went out. He felt sick again and prayed he wouldn't vomit in the back seat.

A voice came from the front seat. "We need your military I.D. and your liberty pass or leave papers."

O'Bryan was hunched forward on the back seat with his head in his hands. He raised slightly. "Don't have my papers. Someone robbed me, hit me on the head."

"Save it, jarhead, every drunk marine we find claims someone did something to him. Did they pour that booze down your throat? Where you stationed, Camp Pendleton?"

"No, Vietnam, on leave from Vietnam, Twenty-sixth Marines."

There was a moment of silence from the front seat. The only sound was a low grumble from the driver's stomach.

"You goin' back to Vietnam?"

"Yes, goin' back in thirty days."

"Shit, Hall, this kid's goin' back to Vietnam. Son, every jarhead we arrest is always just goin' to Vietnam. What do you think, partner?"

Hal lit a cigarette and half turned to look at O'Bryan in the back seat. "Well I'm hungry. If we take him we'll be tied up for at least an hour. Probably have to take him to the hospital too. Son, you got anyone we can call around here to come and get you?"

O'Bryan reached in his shirt pocket and pulled out his I.D. and the letter from Susan Williams. He looked up at the broken outline of the two cops in the front seat. "Please don't put me in jail. I didn't do anything wrong."

"Slide it over the top of the screen."

O'Bryan was still very dizzy and it took a supreme effort to reach up and slide the letter between the top of the mesh screen and the car's headliner."

"We just asked you for I.D. and a number, not a whole damned letter."

"Number is there."

Officer Hal quickly read the letter from Susan Williams. He finished and looked at O'Bryan again. This time his voice was much softer. "Don't worry, me and my partner ain't goin' to take you to jail. Read this," he said and shoved the letter to his partner. "I know where these apartments are at. Hell, lets take him over there."

O'Bryan lay down on the back seat and concentrated on not getting sick. Twenty minutes later the patrol car pulled up in front of Apt. 215 on Rolling Wood Court.

Susan Williams had just arrived home. She had been

out drinking with girlfriends and felt happy and numb. It had occurred to her tonight that she had been doing this too often since her brother's death. But the drinks killed the pain.

Her roommate was gone for the Christmas break and she had to celebrate final exams. She was reaching to unbutton her blouse when the doorbell rang.

She looked through the peephole and saw an L.A.P.D. uniform. Her first thought was the old lady downstairs, but she didn't even have her stereo on. She conjured up her most sober voice. "Who is it?"

"Police officer, I need to talk to a Miss Susan Williams."

She opened the door rebuttoning the top two buttons on her blouse. "I'm Susan Williams, Officer, what can I do for you?"

Officer Hal handed the letter and I.D. to her.

"We got the marine you wrote this letter to out here in the car. He's in pretty bad shape. Claims he's been robbed, but I think he may be drunk."

Susan quickly recognized the name. "His name O'Bryan, John O'Bryan?"

"Not sure, miss, you can come out here and take a look at him."

"Just a minute, let me put some shoes on."

Susan hurried to her bedroom and slipped on a pair of house shoes. She turned on the light and pulled a shoe box from under her bed. It contained letters and pictures her brother had sent from Vietnam. She found the one she was searching for. Doug stood next to a tall, deeply tanned, young marine in front of a bunker. On the back was one of his usual cryptic captions. "Me and John when we lived in the back of the Greta Garbo home for wayward boys and girls."

She ran back to the door with picture in hand, then followed Officer Hal down a flight of stairs to the parking lot.

Hal opened the back door. "He's not a pretty sight."

O'Bryan lay curled in a ball, pretending to be passed out on the back seat. Hal's partner in the front seat shined a flashlight on him and Susan bent down with the photo to compare. It was him. "Is he going to be OK? What's wrong with him?"

"We think he's alright, ma'am. He has a bump and a cut on the back of his head, and he has been drinking. If you don't take him we have no choice but to put him in jail. We just can't leave him laying around."

The cool night air and the police were clearing Susan's head. She felt herself growing more sober by the second. "He was a friend of my brother in Vietnam. I really don't know him that well."

"I know, miss, I read the letter. We really don't want to lock him up. It was either you or jail. They frown on them being arrested in the Marines."

Susan let out a deep breath. "OK, OK, I'll take him. Do I need to take him to the hospital?"

"I don't think so, miss. Try to keep him awake or check on him for the next four to six hours. Just in case he might have a concussion."

The officers, one on either side, half carried O'Bryan up the flight of steps to the apartment. Susan directed them to her roommate's bed and they deposited him there.

They quickly started for the door. "Thank you, miss, the boy will appreciate it when he comes to. Seems like a nice kid, but if he gives you any trouble at all, just call

Hollywood Division and tell them to send unit Three Baker Two. We'll come right back and get him."

She heard one of them ask the other what he wanted to eat as they walked down the stairway. "Goodnight," she said and closed the door.

She turned and walked to the doorway of her roommate's bedroom. O'Bryan lurched towards her. She stepped back and let out a small scream.

"Bathroom, bathroom."

She grabbed him by the arm and shoved him down the hallway to the apartment bathroom. She stood at the door and watched him become violently ill.

She waited until he had finished then wet a towel and handed it to him.

O'Bryan wiped his face and looked at her. "Susan," was all that escaped from him.

"Yes?"

"I'm sorry, really sorry. I didn't plan on meeting you like this."

"It's OK. How do you feel, better now?"

"A little bit. Some bikers robbed me tonight. I didn't want to come here like this."

"They didn't give you much choice."

"I feel so dumb. I tried to call you a couple of times today. I have a hotel room."

"I've been out all evening with some friends. Come on in the living room and sit down. I'll make some coffee.

O'Bryan followed her down the hallway to the living room. He kept one hand pressed against the wall to steady himself. He felt very dizzy again. "Susan, can I just lay down for a minute? I am so tired."

She stopped, turned and led him back to the bedroom.

He lay on the bed and she sat next to him. She felt a strong wave of pity for him. *I've seen stay dogs in better shape.* She took the towel and wiped his face. "Don't worry about a thing, take it easy."

She sat there for a few minutes and knew he was asleep from his slow steady breathing in the dark. She looked at him in the dim light from the hallway. He looked so young but she knew from Doug's letters they were close to the same age. Where was his family? Where was his home? There would be plenty of time later to ask questions.

She stood and took the towel back to the bathroom, then went to the kitchen and fixed a stiff Seagram's and 7 Up. She sat on the sofa and looked at the photo of her brother on the end table. He smiled that silly smile of his wearing that outrageous Marine Barracks Hat. She sat O'Bryan's I.D. and the letter next to the photo.

She downed the drink quickly and fixed another, looked at her watch and was surprised to see that it was 3 a.m. The police had said to check him for the next few hours.

She walked back to the bedroom and the smell of the soiled uniform greeted her at the door. There was only one thing to do. She removed the shirt first and after some thought, his shoes, socks and pants. She opened the bedroom window and a breeze began to blow across the room. She pulled back the bedspread and he stirred slightly when she covered him with a sheet.

She went to the bathroom, filled the sink with water and put his uniform in to soak. She then changed into her nightshirt and decided she would check him once more before she went to bed.

*   *   *

O'Bryan opened his eyes and saw only moonlight coming through the bedroom window. He sensed someone in the room and saw her standing motionless, wearing a blue satin nightshirt at the end of the bed. A cool breeze blew in from the slightly raised window and lightly flowed across his body. *She must have undressed me.* The night was a confused collage of consciousness which slipped in and out without notice.

He thought that he must surely be dreaming and closed his eyes again. Susan went to the bathroom and rinsed out the soiled shirt and hung it on hangers over the tub. She then went and fixed another stiff drink, but was only able to down half of it. She felt so tired, but she walked to the bedroom again. This time she decided to lay across the foot of the bed. She intended to rest there for just a minute.

CHAPTER SEVEN

Sun filtered through the bedroom curtains and small white dots of light played across O'Bryan's face. He wiped his hands across his eyes and sat up in bed.

His mouth had an acid taste and his head throbbed. He smelled a faint odor of perfume and hair spray which popped his bloodshot eyes wide open.

She lay across the bottom of the bed on her stomach. A thick veil of dark hair hid her face, but he knew it was Susan Williams and that last night was not a bad dream. He rubbed his eyes just in case there was a chance she might disappear.

He heard a small but very definite snore issue from under the hair in time with her breathing. The blue nightshirt had ridden up over her bottom to reveal a matching pair of blue satin panties. He rubbed his forehead and looked up at the white ceiling.

He raised the covers and was relieved to see that he still had on his skivvies. He sat very still with his eyes closed. The events of the previous night ran together in his mind. The more he remembered the worse he felt.

The smell of perfume assaulted him again and he opened his eyes. He looked down at the sleeping girl and traced the leg bent towards him from her polished toes, to a faint tan line, to a mound of blue satin. *Could we have had sex? No, I would remember that! Holy shit, Doug's sister, what am I doing here?*

He slowly eased from the side of the bed, picked up his shoes and socks, then padded softly out to the hall and gently closed the door behind him.

O'Bryan found his damp uniform shirt and pants hanging in the bathroom and eased into them. He stopped and looked at himself in the bathroom mirror. He decided that he looked about like the survivor of a shipwreck.

He knew that he owed Susan for saving him last night, but he was just too ashamed to face her right now. He rubbed the black stubble on his chin. Why had she crawled in there on the end of the bed? His head hurt and he decided he would explore that later.

He walked down the small hallway across the living room/dining area and decided he should at least leave a note.

He looked around the room for something to write with. Sitting on the coffee table next to a picture of Doug and his I.D., was an empty fifth of Seagram's and a watered-down drink. He bent and picked up the card.

Must not have been feeling any pain herself, he thought.

He found a note pad and pencil on the breakfast bar next to the telephone.

Dear Susan,

Thanks for bailing me out of the jam last night. I owe you at least a dinner for that, if you still want to talk to me. I really feel dumb about the whole mess. It's not the way I wanted to meet you or your parents. I know Doug would just say I screwed up again. Please don't mention last night and give me a chance to try this all over again. Call me at the Biltmore downtown when you're up and around.

Thanks,
O'Bryan

He pulled the door to and locked it behind him as he left. He squinted in the bright morning sunlight and held tight to the railing until he reached the bottom of the stairs.

After a brief search he found the manager's office and persuaded him to call him a taxi. The manager told him to wait outside for the cab.

The taxi driver demanded O'Bryan give him his military I.D. card when he explained that his money was in the hotel safe. Even when they arrived, the driver insisted on following him to the hotel desk. "I been stiffed by too many young jarheads," he explained.

It seemed to O'Bryan that no one trusted anyone very much in this town. After the last 24 hours he was beginning to understand why.

He was happy to be back in his room. He locked the door and took a long hot bath. He dried off and crawled between the crisp hotel sheets and wondered how much money the men in his squad would pay to trade places with him. He fell asleep with that thought and a smile.

Six hours later the phone rang in his room. He reached for the nightstand by instinct and picked up the receiver.

"Hello."

"John O'Bryan?"

"Yeah."

"This is Susan, I'm pretty put out with you."

"Just a second."

O'Bryan paused for a moment and shook his head. "You have a right to be. I should have never given those cops your address. I apologize."

"No, I'm not mad about that. If I didn't want to help you I would have said so. Where did you go this morning?"

"I got a cab and went back to the hotel. I needed to get cleaned up."

"You could have cleaned up here."

"I had put you through enough trouble."

"Were your clothes dry? I was going to take them down to the laundromat when I got up."

O'Bryan smiled. "They were a little damp."

"Are you hungry?"

"I'm starved."

"Good, you're invited to my parents' for one of my mother's famous spaghetti dinners. They are really looking forward to meeting you."

"Sounds great."

"I'll pick you up in two hours, in front of the hotel. I'll be in a red Corvair."

"Thanks," said O'Bryan and he hung up the phone.

He bounced out of bed and felt none the worse for wear. He guessed that all was forgiven with Susan. Still, he was glad he had left this morning. It was just too uncomfortable.

He shaved, dressed in a clean uniform and treated himself to a short shopping spree at a men's clothing store three blocks away.

In two hours he stood in front of the Biltmore wearing a new pair of gray slacks, and a blue oxford shirt.

He waited next to the curb and rocked nervously on his heels as he rehearsed what he might say to them about their son's death. *It was over in an instant. He never knew what hit him. No, I wouldn't lie. No one knows what it feels like to be blown apart. I'll simply tell them what happened.*

A red Corvair pulled to the curb next to him. He bent to look at her and she waved to him. He opened the passenger door and got in. She smiled a familiar crooked smile at him and there was no doubt that he was looking at Doug Williams's sister.

"You look a hundred percent better than you did last night. How do you feel?"

"A hundred percent better, except I'm hungry."

"Great, let's go."

She eased the car away from the curb and into the traffic. Soon the tall buildings were gone and they were another link in a seemingly endless chain of freeway traffic. He admired the way she handled the little car.

"Is traffic always this bad?"

"Oh it's not bad now, you should see it during rush hour. You're from Oklahoma, aren't you?"

"Yeah."

"What's it like there?"

"Where I'm from it's pretty small and quiet compared to all this. I just can't get used to seeing all these palm trees at Christmas time."

"Are you going home for Christmas, be with the family?"

"No, my mom's dead and me and my dad don't get along."

"I'm sorry."

"It's OK, it was all a long time ago. At least it seems that way. I got a little sister, talked to her on the phone. She lives with an aunt and uncle."

"Are you going to go see her?"

"No, but I got to find her something for Christmas."

"If you can't find it out here, then it's probably not for sale."

"I know, I just need to call her back and pin her down. Find out exactly what she wants."

"Don't worry, you find out what she wants and I'll show you where to find it. What do you do for fun back home?"

"Nothing special, go to a movie, hang out with friends. I used to like to hunt, but I don't know anymore. How much farther?"

"We'll be there soon. We take highway 91 to the Riverside Freeway and get off on the Santa Ana exit."

O'Bryan nodded, but the directions meant nothing to him. "I thought your family lived in Anaheim."

She laughed, "They do."

"Oh."

The scenery began to change. He could see a few large homes and neat manicured lawns set back away from the freeway.

"Doug wrote me about your girlfriend in his last letter. Have you had a chance to patch that up?"

"No, I haven't tried to. She made her choice. Can't really blame her. It's a long time for someone to sit around and wait."

"I think it's kind of rotten. She could have waited just a little longer."

O'Bryan glanced over at her. She was slowing for the exit ramp and downshifted the little car. She spoke in the same easy manner as her brother.

Her long dark brown hair was parted on one side and swept across her forehead. She wore a blue denim shirt that was tied together at the waist and a pair of blue jeans.

She had not mentioned falling asleep on the bed with him and he would not bring it up. Still, an image of blue satin stirred in the back of his mind.

Soon they were driving down steep slopes on winding residential streets flanked by huge front yards.

The houses varied from two- and three-story monsters to sprawling one-level Spanish style homes. There were stately trees draped with moss and the ever-present palm trees to provide shade.

There was nothing like this in Washita, Oklahoma. O'Bryan knew that Doug Williams had to be the only marine grunt from this neighborhood. He and Doug had never talked much about money. It really had no meaning in their world. Doug must have gone way out of his way to end up in Vietnam, he thought.

Susan finally pulled into the driveway of a large white two-story home. There was a white rail fence around a big front yard and several of those sad trees he had never seen before, draped with the hanging moss.

This was something completely out of his element. He felt he was stepping out in the dead center of people who could either buy or sell him the rest of his life.

She switched off the key. "Here we are."

He bent and looked out the windshield, then back at her. "It's a nice place, looks like the Beaver could live here, and five of his closest friends."

"Not the Cleavers, just me, Doug, Mom and Dad."

They got out of the car and walked along a sidewalk lined with outdoor lights to the front door. Susan opened the tinted glass storm door and then an oversized oak front door with a Christmas holly wreath in the middle.

They stepped inside a spacious tiled foyer and Susan

yelled, "Mom, we're here."

A voice answered from somewhere in the back of the house. "Back here in the Florida room."

Susan led him down a hallway to the back of the house. He stayed close behind her and glanced in doorways as they proceeded. The big house was decorated for Christmas. He caught a glimpse of a fifteen-foot Christmas tree next to a bay window.

Doug also never mentioned what his father did for a living. O'Bryan could only surmise that whatever he did, he did it very well.

They emerged in a room which was full of plants, flowers and wicker furniture. The west wall was all glass and at least twelve feet high.

Susan's mother and father stood in the middle of the room framed by the glass. Over their shoulders in the back yard was the swimming pool he knew must be there.

"John O'Bryan, this is my mother, Fran and my father, Jim."

"Glad to meet you, Mrs. Williams, Mr. Williams."

Susan's mother took his arm. "We have certainly looked forward to meeting you. Doug always mentioned you in his letters. Please sit down. Would you like something to drink?"

Before he could respond Susan volunteered, "I'll get us a couple of Cokes, or would you rather have something else?"

"Coke's fine."

Susan turned and headed out of the room.

O'Bryan sat down in a blue cushioned wicker chair while Jim and Fran Williams sat on a matching love seat across from him.

Jim Williams started. "Susan says you're from Oklahoma?"

"Yes, sir."

"We were in Tulsa once, long time ago, on business. You live close to there?"

"No, sir, down in the middle of the state."

Fran leaned forward. "How long did you know Doug?"

"A little over a year."

"It is so nice of you to come and see us, we really appreciate it."

"It's the least I could do."

O'Bryan could see that she was already struggling to maintain her composure. This was not going to be easy.

Susan returned with the drinks and handed one to him. She sat in another chair next to him and placed two coasters on a glass top table which separated O'Bryan from her parents. Jim Williams took his wife's hand. "How did it happen? Were you there?"

"Yes, sir, we were sweeping through a valley, looking for a North Vietnamese mortar crew that had hit us the day before."

"Was this around Khe Sanh?"

"Yes, sir, in the mountains just north."

"Dad has become kind of an expert about that country."

Fran Williams looked at her husband. "I think it's more of an obsession, an unhealthy one."

"No it's not, I just like to keep up on what's going on over there. I think it's insanity. I'm sorry, son, go on.

"We were sweeping through this valley, it was early in the morning. Doug and I were walking right next to each other. We came to a little hill and I picked up a leech. I stopped to get it off and Doug kept going with the rest of the squad. They were in some real high elephant grass.

Susan interrupted, "What's that?"

"It's like huge blades of grass about six to eight feet high that's sharp as a razor on both sides."

"Oh."

"They went into this elephant grass and I was trying to catch up with them...then there was this explosion and it knocked me down."

Jim Williams leaned forward. "What was it?"

"We figured later that it was a dud 250-pound bomb. Somebody found part of a tail assembly. They set it off with an electric blasting cap. It got the whole squad."

Jim Williams looked down at his feet. Fran Williams had begun to sob now. She had her head in her hands. They were silent little sobs but her whole body shook.

Susan moved to her mother's side and knelt next to her. Tears glistened on the side of her face as she leaned to put her arms around her mother.

O'Bryan sensed himself choking up. He was sorry he had come now. These people needed to get on with their lives and he was only prolonging the grief.

He felt guilty and frustrated with his inability to think of anything to say which would help them.

Jim Williams's voice was husky with outrage when he spoke. "Did you kill any of the little bastards?"

Fran erupted, "Who cares, Jim? What difference does it make?"

Susan stood and took her mother's hand. "Come on, Mom, I know John's hungry. Let's go put dinner on the table."

Fran stood. "Of course he is," and they walked arm in

arm out of the room.

O'Bryan waited until they left the room before replying to Mr. Williams's question. "I don't know if I killed any of them. I saw them, there were three of them. I got a good shot at one of them. There was blood where he had been. I know I hit at least one. That's the way it is over there most of the time. You're lucky to see what you're shooting at."

"Fran's right, son, it really doesn't make much difference. Doug's gone whether you killed one or a hundred. I have about decided that the only thing that does make sense is to stop all of it. So no one else has to go through this."

"I feel the same sometimes, but it's my job. We go where we're sent and do what they want us to do."

"I know, but I bet your folks feel the same way I do. I never really thought about it until this happened. Now, I am beginning to wonder just exactly what my son died for. Are we fighting to win or just not to lose? I don't think I could ever forgive this government if it turned out that he died for nothing. If they wasted his life."

O'Bryan sat silent. The smell of spaghetti and garlic bread wafted by him. His stomach rumbled. Jim Williams had asked the question he feared most.

"Dinner is served," shouted Susan from the doorway.

O'Bryan stood quickly, relieved by the interruption. Jim Williams rose and put his arm around John's shoulder. "Come on, let's eat."

CHAPTER EIGHT

They sat in the formal dining room. A splendid crystal chandelier reflected off the cherry wood dining table, which seated twelve. Jim Williams sat at the head of the table with his wife at his right, his daughter and O'Bryan on his left.

Fran Williams took great pleasure watching O'Bryan devour her spaghetti in the place where her son had always sat. "Susan tells me that you are going to be in town for the holidays."

"Yes, ma'am."

"Then you must share Christmas with us. That is, if you have no other plans."

"Mom puts on a great Christmas dinner. I must gain ten pounds every December."

"Well, I am not positive I'll be in town, but if I am, you got a deal."

"I am going to have Susan keep track of you and if I find out you are in town I'll be very upset if you aren't here for dinner."

"People just think the F.B.I. is tough. They never had Mom on their trail."

O'Bryan ate more than he thought he possibly could. He had nearly forgotten how good a home cooked meal could be. Fran Williams kept filling his plate.

"You're much too thin," she said. "What do they feed you boys over there?"

He noticed she avoided using the word Vietnam. "They're called C-rations, Mrs. Williams, and I can't discuss them while we are eating."

Jim Williams pushed back from the table and lit a cigarette. "When do you have to go back?"

"My leave is up January the 14th," replied O'Bryan, who had decided he couldn't eat another bite.

"Ready for desert?"

"No thank you, I simply couldn't."

"Well it's chocolate cake, I'll wrap a piece for you to take with you."

Susan looked at her watch. "Dad I'm going to take him to the moratorium service tonight. We have to move or we're going to be late."

This was news to O'Bryan. "What's a moratorium service?"

"It's kind of a meeting to remember the men who have died in Vietnam and a way to say we want the killing to stop."

"Sounds like a good deal to me."

Susan stood up and O'Bryan rose from his chair.

Fran Williams also stood. "No one goes anywhere until I get John his cake."

John, Susan and her father stood at the front door awaiting Fran.

"Thank you for the dinner, Mr. Williams, it was great."

"It was our pleasure. And remember what we said about Christmas."

"I'll remember. I never turn down an invitation to eat."

Fran returned with some cake wrapped in aluminum foil. She got on her tiptoes and gave him a kiss on the cheek goodbye. "Be careful and stay in touch."

"I will."

When they were in the car he turned to Susan. "I am so full, I hope I don't go to sleep during this moratorium service."

"I don't think you will. Some friends of mine will be there that I want you to meet."

She backed out of the drive and turned on the car's headlights. The sun was beginning to set. O'Bryan hoped she would drive more slowly than she had on the way out.

"Where is this thing at?"

"The Federal Building downtown. Not far from where you're staying."

"Who's putting this on?"

"It's kind of a political club at school. It's called Students for a Democratic Society. Ever hear of it?"

"No, I don't think I've heard of it."

She reached and turned on the car radio. The Mamas and the Papas sang California Dreamin' and he dutifully closed his eyes and held his stomach with both hands.

They arrived downtown at dusk. A crowd of about 500 had already gathered. Susan was forced to park the Corvair six blocks from the Federal Building.

She quickly locked the car and hurried on in front of him.

"Now some of these guys are a little strange, but when you get to know them, they're a lot of fun."

"What do you mean by strange?"

"I mean they may look unusual since you have been in the Service and out of the country for awhile."

He could hear someone in the distance shouting, "Peace now, peace now."

"There aren't very many of us here tonight," she said over her shoulder as they headed up the sidewalk. "Christmas Break."

The looming concrete and steel buildings looked

forsaken. The bottom floors were all dark. The blue tint given off by the street lights mixed with the orange haze from the setting sun to form a color in the air he had never seen. Strung between the light poles with this garish backdrop were Christmas decorations, which reminded him more of Halloween than "Seasons Greetings."

He purposely slowed his pace but had to speed up again for fear of losing her in the crowd.

People ahead of them carried signs that read "Honk For Peace." In response, cars honked their horns and flashed their headlights as they passed by. Up ahead, a police barricade forced the traffic to detour around the block.

It all reminded O'Bryan of a carnival he had been to when he was small. He had gotten separated from his mother and was terrified. He had cried and cried but no one had paid any attention to him. Finally a woman took him to a police officer and they had walked around until he had found his frantic mother. He remembered the fascination and fright of the loud noise and bright colors.

He followed Susan past a line of about twenty bored cops at the road block. "Don't worry," she said, "We have a permit for the demonstration." Her voice trailed off and she stopped to stand on her tiptoes. "I don't see anyone yet that I know."

They worked their way around the edge of the crowd in the street, to the front of the Federal Building. He noted there were some type of guards stationed at the front of each glass door entrance.

He also noticed a man with a camera filming the crowd from a fourth floor window across the street. He was glad he had not worn his uniform. He wondered if anyone else had noticed the man partially hidden by a curtain in the window. If he were a sniper they would all be dead meat.

A figure in a black Halloween death costume complete with a scythe stood thirty feet away, by the center entrance to the building. Next to him stood a boy of about nineteen or twenty with shoulder length brown hair.

He wore a gray sweatshirt with "STOP THE DRAFT" emblazoned on the front and a black armband. He held a microphone, which led to a public address speaker.

This is where the "peace now" had come from. Susan had stopped walking. O'Bryan decided this must be the center of the "happening."

"That's Dean in the costume," said Susan. "I've seen him in it before in a street play on campus."

O'Bryan nodded.

The sunset faded. A girl with a guitar stepped up to the microphone. In an exquisite high voice she began to sing. "Where have all the flowers gone, long time passing? Where have all the flowers gone, long time ago?"

People in the crowd began to sing along. Susan lit both candles with her cigarette lighter and passed it on, where it disappeared in the crowd.

O'Bryan stood silent for a moment with the candle and listened to voices he knew would never speak again. Anger grew inside him and his fingers sunk into the sides of the candle.

At the feet of the boy in the death costume were two metal bowls. When a breeze snaked through the crowd O'Bryan thought he caught the faint scent of lighter fluid.

The girl finished the song and the crowd applauded her performance. The "peace now" boy pulled the microphone back and it was clear he was the master of ceremonies.

"We are gathered here tonight to send a message to our government. The message is short and unmistakable. Stop the killing in Vietnam. The United States is financing the wholesale slaughter of oppressed, innocent men, women, and children. The most effective way for us to stop this genocide is to refuse to be a part of it."

With that the speaker pulled a small white card from his back pocket. "Death" or Dean bent down, picked up one of the metal bowls and held it in front of him.

The speaker began again, "This is the blood of the oppressed which is on the hands of our country." He dipped the card into the blood and held it up to the crowd.

Someone threw a match into the other bowl and the liquid ignited. "Pass up your cards," shouted the speaker. He then bent and dropped his card into the fire.

The crowd began to cheer and someone in the front row unfurled a homemade North Vietnamese flag.

O'Bryan's body went rigid. His grip tightened on the candle and the white wax oozed between his fingers. Hot wax from the top of the candle dripped along his hand but he didn't feel it.

His thoughts were focused on whether or not he could reach the bowl of alleged blood and pour it over the speaker's head. He decided that he could but he would never make it out of the crowd.

It wasn't that he hated the North Vietnamese. He wanted to stop this profanity of the dead. These people, his own countrymen, were the ones he held in contempt. He strained to stand still.

He doubted the bowl was filled with human blood. He couldn't imagine the people in this crowd bleeding for anyone else, not even each other.

The whole thing was so contrived. He even doubted there were very many real draft cards being burned. His eyes swept the crowd. These were for the most part, middle class kids who probably spent a good deal of money to appear poor.

O'Bryan smelled the pungent odor of marijuana. He turned and spotted the source. A guy four people back with long blond hair, wearing a Marine Corps dress blue jacket, holding a wine bottle and a marijuana cigarette.

The candle snapped in half in his hand and the burning end dropped to the ground. A girl standing next to him wearing combat boots ground it into the pavement.

He bent down to Susan Williams's ear. "What a bunch of assholes. Why don't they just say they are afraid to go?"

She looked at him, her eyes wide with disbelief. "You don't understand."

"I understand all I need to know about this."

He turned and began to shove his way out of the crowd. She called after him but he ignored her. The speaker began to recite the names of the dead from California.

O'Bryan paused at the edge of the crowd to see if Susan Williams would follow him. She stood in the front of the crowd where he had left her. He guessed she was waiting for them to recite her brother's name in the litany of the dead. His eyes burned a little from smog as he swept them across the crowd.

The boy with the marine dress blue tunic emerged on the other side of the gathering walking quickly across the street. Blond hair bounced on the boy's shoulders as he trotted the last few steps into an alleyway and disappeared into shadows.

The boy was tall and about the same age as O'Bryan. The dress blue tunic did not fit well. The sleeves stopped well above his wrists. He sat his wine bottle down, then leaned against the brick wall of a building and unbuttoned his jeans in the darkness of the alley. The names of the dead servicemen mixed with the sound of urine splashing on the brick wall.

The boy never heard a sound as O'Bryan's arm snaked around his neck from behind. O'Bryan had perfected his technique in the hills around Khe Sanh on moonless nights.

This time instead of a knife, O'Bryan slashed with the straight bone above his wrist to his victims throat, then choked him bending the boy backwards until the blond head slumped and the long legs went limp.

O'Bryan laid the unconscious boy gently on his back, them removed the dress blue jacket. The attack had taken less than ninety seconds. He knew the boy would come to soon. He quickly folded the jacket under his arm and said softly, "Sorry, but you don't rate to wear this, asshole."

O'Bryan emerged from the alleyway and walked away from the crowd in the general direction of his hotel. He felt giddy and thought he heard Doug Williams's name echo down the street after him.

Chapter Nine

O'Bryan lay on his back in the big hotel bed, fully clothed, his eyes staring at the ceiling. It had taken him nearly two hours to make his way back to the hotel. The first hour he spent walking aimlessly on downtown streets until he was propositioned by a hooker who gave him directions back to the hotel.

He ran the events of the evening over in his mind trying to decide whether he would call Susan Williams again or simply let all this slide away and leave town. While mentally connecting the little holes in the white acoustic tile ceiling he decided that in the morning he would check on a flight to Oklahoma City and go try to find some old friends in Washita. Having decided that, he felt very tired and fell asleep while trying to see faces of friends in the dotted ceiling.

He was back in Vietnam on a mine sweep along Route 9. He could see a marine in the front of a staggered column swinging a flat round metal detector from side to side. The copper-brown dirt road curved away from him to the right and he could see the front of a large arched wooden bridge. To the right of the bridge were familiar buildings. He stopped walking and other marines stepped around him continuing toward the bridge. It was Washita, Oklahoma. The patrol was going to cross the bridge and he would be home. Only another hundred yards: he ran to catch up. Two cracks sounded and the lead marine with the metal detector slumped to the ground. He heard four consecutive thumps in the distance and knew it was incoming mortars. All he had to do was make it to the bridge and he would be home and safe. The mortar rounds exploded around him and marines screamed in agony as red clouds of dust billowed up from the explosions.

The impacting mortar rounds began to walk slowly towards him. He ran low with all his might but seemed to go nowhere. He looked up and saw three North Vietnamese gun crews firing the mortars from the middle of Washita. It was a trap. A girl's voice called his name over the din of the mortar fire. "O'Bryan, O'Bryan!"

He screamed and sat up in bed, his ears ringing. Some one was pounding on his door and yelling his name.

"O'Bryan, O'Bryan, open up. It's Susan."

He sat up slowly on the bed and looked at his watch, one a.m. He walked slowly to the hotel room door and unlocked it. His shirt stuck to his back, damp with dream sweat. Susan Williams stood in the doorway holding a brown grocery sack. "Can I come in?"

"Sure," O'Bryan muttered stepping out of her way.

She stepped quickly across the threshold and asked over her shoulder, "Got any ice?"

"There's some down the hall, a machine inside a closet."

She turned and looked up at him. "Where did you run off to? I looked all over for you. I called here twice."

"Sorry, I just couldn't stick around there. It was a little too intense."

She nodded her head up and down. "No, I'm sorry, I really shouldn't have taken you to that, but I just wanted you to meet some of my friends."

"It's OK, I'm over it. Do you mind if I take a quick shower. I fell asleep for a little while and I feel like I have cobwebs in my head."

"Sure, go ahead," she replied. "Just give me your ice bucket and I'll fix us a couple of drinks while you're in there. I want a chance to talk to you about Doug and the war without my parents around."

O'Bryan walked to the bathroom and retrieved a metal ice bucket. Susan set the grocery sack on a round table in the middle of the room. "I brought bourbon and vodka."

O'Bryan leaned out the bathroom doorway and tossed the ice bucket across the room. She made a fumbling two-hand catch. "Good hands," he said.

She smiled. "Used to be a shortstop. I got Coke, 7 Up, or orange juice, so what'll it be?"

O'Bryan leaned against the bathroom doorway and thought for a few seconds. "Bourbon and Coke," he said and closed the door.

Susan paused at the doorway, took off a shoe and placed it at the bottom of the door, so it wouldn't close behind her. "Back in a minute," she said disappearing down the hallway.

O'Bryan emerged quickly from behind the bathroom door and sprinted to the closet. He pulled out his seabag and reached inside it. He pulled out a new set of white skivvies. He smiled to himself. *In case there's an accident here.* He also grabbed a new light blue oxford shirt, still in the cellophane package and a new pair of blue slacks from a closet hanger, then turned and dashed back to the bathroom. The hot shower stung his back as steam filled the bathroom.

In a few minutes he could hear the sound of television playing over the water. He tried to guess from the voices what show she was watching. After a minute he gave up. It had been over a year since he had watched TV. *No telling what people are watching now.*

He backed under the shower and let the full force of the water hit the base of his neck. *What does she want with me, why did she come all the way over here and bring booze with her?* An image of her sprawled across the bed at her apartment with her nightshirt hiked to reveal creamy white legs and a blue satin mound flashed in his mind.

He reprimanded himself for being aroused. *You asshole, she's just trying to be nice to a friend of her dead brother. Probably feels sorry for you. Be nice to her.'* He looked down. *And stop thinking with that.* Whatever the reason, he was glad for the company of a girl. If it was just pity then he would take that.

He dried off quickly, brushed his teeth, inspected his face and decided against shaving again. He opened a new bottle of English Leather cologne and splashed it liberally on his face and arms. He pulled on the crisp new shirt and slacks and joined her in the room.

Susan Williams was seated with her legs curled under her in a big blue high back chair, next to a small oval table by the window. She got up and walked across to the TV set and switched it off. O'Bryan walked to a matching chair on the other side of the table and sat down.

There was a drink she had prepared for him on the table. "Hope that's not too watered down by now," she said returning to her chair.

"No, it's fine," he said between sips.

His eyes traversed the room searching for the dress blue tunic he had taken from the boy at the demonstration. He had set it in the chair where she was now sitting. It now hung in the open closet on a hotel hanger.

She pulled her chair around to the front of the round coffee table so that she now faced him at a forty-five-degree angle.

"First of all, I want to apologize for taking you to the moratorium tonight."

"That's OK, you don't need to."

"Yes, I do. I think that was a little too much for someone just home. I shouldn't have taken you."

"I'm a big boy. I didn't like what I saw, so I left."

Susan sipped her drink and then answered, "Well, those things can sometimes get out of hand and do attract some strange people. One poor guy tonight got beaten and robbed right after you left." O'Bryan smiled and watched the puzzled look on her face.

"It's not funny, you know, I knew the guy and he was attacked for no reason."

"I didn't rob him, he just didn't rate the uniform," he said pointing to the closet.

"That was you? That was his?"

He nodded yes twice and sipped his drink.

"John, you just can't go around doing things like that. The man has a right to his opinion."

"Maybe so, but I just didn't like the way he dressed his opinion." He looked straight at her over the rim of his glass. Searching her face for a reaction.

She sighed, "Come on, lighten up. Where did you go after you left me?"

"I just walked around for awhile. It was kind of nice, just walking at night, not having to worry about ambushes or mines or anything. What happened to you?"

"You mean after you disappeared?"

"Yeah."

"First, I looked around for you. After I finally gave that up, I went with some friends over to a little get together. I was hoping you would come with me."

"Some of your friends from S.D.S.?"

"Yes, I called your room three times. No one answered. I was starting to get a little worried. I see I shouldn't have."

"Did they read Doug's name off?"

"Yes, I started to cry." She paused and looked down. "I wish you had stayed."

O'Bryan sat back with his drink. His stomach began to feel warm as the alcohol started to take effect and embolden him. "Why did you leave your friends and come over here?"

"I told you, I was worried, besides, you seemed so sad tonight. I thought you needed a little cheering up. I'm sure the party is still going."

"I think I'll pass on the party. I just feel like I don't fit in with your friends."

She finished her drink and set it down, then leaned toward him. "That's not fair. You really don't know them."

"You're right," he said, not wanting to argue.

She held out her hand, "Ready for another?"

"I'm fine," he said, lifting the hotel glass.

She got up, walked to the dresser where the ice buckets and bottles sat and began to fix herself another vodka and orange juice.

"You know, technically, we have slept together and I don't really know much about you. Your name's John O'Bryan. You were my brother's best friend and you're from some little town in Oklahoma, where you have an ex-girlfriend." She turned, walked back to her chair and sat down.

"That's about it," he said.

She took a deep drink of the vodka and orange juice. "No, no, you don't get off that easy. Start at the top. So who's John O'Bryan?"

He squirmed in his chair, uneasy with her scrutiny.

"I think I will fix another," he said rising and walking over to the ice and mix.

She smiled a winsome look at him. "Let's have it."

He walked back, set his fresh drink on the table and looked down at her. "Do I get to ask the same questions?"

"Sure," she said, "if you want to."

He sat down and thought a moment. "You mean like define John O'Bryan?"

"That's it."

"I'm not sure I know, to be truthful."

"Not too many people do," she said standing.

He was surprised to see she had already finished her second drink and was on her way to fix a third.

He was warming to the game. "I can tell you who he was."

She returned to her chair and pulled it closer facing him. "OK, I'll settle for that."

He sat back and traced the top of the rim of his glass with a finger. "He was a seventeen-year-old kid whose family broke up when he was fourteen. He got his drunken father to sign an enlistment waiver so he could join the Marines after his junior year. He needed a place to sleep, food to eat and clothes to wear. He signed a contract. The Marine Corps kept their end of the deal, shipped him to Vietnam when he was eighteen. They pay him very little, work him long hours and expect him to risk his life whenever it's deemed necessary."

He paused and looked up at her. "It's a sad but common story."

"Doesn't sound like too good a deal to me," she said propping her chin on her hand. "Do you hate being in the Marines?"

"No, not really, there are certain other fringe benefits."

"Such as?"

"If I live through this, with the money I save while in Vietnam and the G.I. Bill, I'll get a chance to go to college and get an education.

He burst out laughing.

"What's so funny?" she asked. "That's an awful big IF."

"I was just thinking that I'll be on a war scholarship, or should I call it a scholar war-ship." He began to chuckle again.

She studied him with mock intensity. "Made yourself laugh again," she said sipping her drink. "Sounds to me like you're gambling with your life."

He stood up quickly and made a motion with his right hand as if rolling a pair of dice. "Hold that thought," he said, then walked to the dresser and fixed another bourbon and Coke. As he returned he was aware that her eyes followed him carefully across the room. He sat and leaned toward her.

"There's something else. Remember I told you that when I was eighteen they shipped me to Vietnam?"

"Yeah."

"The reason is that Congress decided," he did his best imitation of Lyndon Johnson, "an American boy can't officially be killed until he is eighteen."

"Her eyebrows arched. "How benevolent of them."

"Well there was a big group of us waiting to turn eighteen after we finished boot camp and infantry training. I called it the baby Marine Corps. Most of them were hardcore juvenile delinquents, like me or worse."

She laughed, "Sounds like the lost boys in Peter Pan."

"You could say that. I think maybe warfare pre-school is more accurate. There were kids from everywhere, blacks, whites, Puerto Ricans, Indians. They put us all together in these big wooden two-story squad bays at Camp Pendleton. We had an old staff sergeant in charge of us, he's dead now. Got killed on 881 the day before your brother and the rest of the squad got hit."

"Was his name Alvarez?"

"How do you know?"

"Doug mentioned him in a letter."

"Any way, the first day we were there Alvarez fell us all outside in formation at attention. He walked through the ranks and inspected us. Then he went back to the front of the formation and shook his head. He asked us, how many of you people are here because you got in trouble with the law and they gave you a choice of jail or the Marines? I looked around and about half the guys in the formation had their hands raised. Then he asked, how many of you people are here because you got some girl pregnant and had to leave town? Everybody else but me and one other guy raised their hand. He walked back to where I was, got right in my face and yelled, "What the fuck you doin' here boy?""

She smiled and laughed, "Did it make you wonder?"

"I've asked myself that question lots of times. They really had no idea what to do with us."

"What did they have you doing?"

"We spent all day picking up trash and doing close order drill. It was mind-numbing, then one day it dawned on me."

She giggled, "Pray tell, what was that?"

He straightened out his arms in front of him. "We all belonged now, we were counted. If something happened to one of us, we would be missed. You know, a marine never leaves another wounded marine, all that stuff."

"Ever read any sociology?"

He shook his head no.

"Sounds to me like you were in a government-sponsored juvenile gang."

"No," he said, "Don't you see, the Marine Corps had become our giant green parent." They both began to laugh again. He liked her smile and the way her head tilted when she laughed.

"I hope you know," she said reaching and touching his arm, "there is something very Freudian about this giant green parent talk and all of you running around with these long phallic symbols."

He looked genuinely concerned. "I never thought of that."

"This is getting pretty deep," she said, "I better fix us both another drink." She picked up his glass and walked to the dresser. "Keep talking, I'm listening."

"I've said about enough," he replied. "What about you?"

She walked back and handed him a fresh drink and smiled. "I think you may be a disturbed young man—interesting, but disturbed. Drink this and call me in the morning."

"Thank you, doctor, for the drink, I know I'm

disturbed. But how many people will hire a seventeen-year-old, train him and trust him with the lives of his fellow workers?"

She screwed up her nose in exasperation. "Don't you see? They are taking advantage of you, and people like you who find themselves in trouble."

"I don't see it that way."

She looked him level in the eye. "All they want is your warm body behind a gun."

He thought her eyes were beautiful; his head was spinning. "There's something else," he started, then paused looking for the right words. "In return for that you get something money can't buy, it's...it's a certain self-respect."

She didn't answer. He knew she must be feeling the effects of the booze too. He noticed her legs had been a little wobbly coming back from the dresser. She seemed to be studying her hands which now held the drink in her lap. She curled her bare feet under her legs.

He broke the silence. "What you said about gambling with my life?"

"Yes."

"I think we all gamble every day, but I think life should be judged solely on quality not quantity."

"Spoken like a true philosopher, Mr. O'Bryan."

"No really, I've thought about it. I'm not afraid of dying. From the little I've seen so far it must be much less painful than living. I just don't like the getting killed part."

She laughed and lifted her glass in salute. "You may be right about quality versus quantity."

"All right," he said, "now that's all there is to me. It's your turn for show and tell."

"Compared to your story, mine's much too boring."

"I'll be the judge of that."

She studied the ceiling for a moment. "OK, I'm twenty-one, a college student who's lived all her life in sunny California. I am majoring in business and plan to go into advertising work."

"I'm impressed," he nodded.

"As well you should be."

"Tell me about your family."

"My dad is a lawyer and Mom is, well you met her, a mom."

"Got any romantic interest?" he said softly.

She considered this for a moment. "There is one person I've kind of been dating regular. He's in his first year of law school. We met at school two years ago." She stopped and studied his face for a reaction. She could see nothing.

"Is it serious?" he asked.

"I'm not sure, it could be."

"What's his name?"

"Tom, Tom Parkhurst. His dad's a lawyer, kind of following in the family tradition."

"How's he kept from being drafted?"

"He's in a reserve unit. Why so curious about him? I thought we were discussing me."

"Sorry, go ahead."

"That's alright, right now I am intoxicated and sleepy. Tell me about Doug again."

"I already told you about Doug."

She leaned forward. "Please, is that the way it really happened? My parents aren't here. You don't have to dress it up. I just want the truth about it."

He looked at her closely. Tears were beginning to form at the corners of her eyes. "That's the way it happened."

"I hate the fucking war," she screamed, and then buried her head in her hands. In a moment she recovered and wiped her eyes with the back of her hand. She smiled at him. "Sorry, not very good company, am I. Here I came over to cheer you up and I'm the one crying in my booze."

"Forget it," he said, "I'll get you some tissue."

He got up and made an effort to walk in a straight line to the bathroom, where he fetched a complimentary box from the vanity. When he returned she was standing in the middle of the room.

She held her arms out and turned slowly around. "This is such a nice big room. Must be costing you a fortune. Whoops," she giggled, holding her hands to her mouth. "Shouldn't say that, not polite."

He handed her the box of tissues. "I don't mind. It is a nice room and it is expensive."

She took two tissues and tossed the box across the room where it landed on the bed.

She wiped her eyes. "Well, got any music in this place?"

"Just a minute," he said crossing to a clock radio on the nightstand next to the bed. He twisted the dial until he found something slow and soft. The Mama's and the Papa's sang "Dedicated to the One I Love."

He walked over to her and bowed elaborately. She pressed against him and he held her delicately, with just his fingertips pressing the small of her back. She relaxed and buried her face into his shoulder.

They moved silently on the carpet to the soft music and paid no notice when the song finished. O'Bryan felt himself being aroused but tried to fight the feeling. There was no use. The smell of her hair and perfume overpowered him. Been gone too long, he thought.

She began to cry again. "I'm sorry, I'm just so dizzy. I'm afraid I'm a real mess."

He guided her toward the bed and when they were close he held her away from him by the shoulders and then sat her on the bed.

"No," she said, looking up at him.

"It's OK, get some rest. It's my turn to take care of you tonight."

She lay back on the thick blue comforter and put her head on one of the pillows. "Just a little while," she said.

He went to the closet and pulled an extra blanket from the shelf. He spread it over her then turned the radio down and sat quietly in a chair across the room. In a few minutes he could hear the even breathing of her sleep.

After a little while he stood, took off his shirt and hung it in the closet. He turned off the light and lay down on the opposite side of the bed, careful not to touch her.

O'Bryan stared at the shadows playing on the ceiling and smiled. The smell of her mixed with the English Leather combined to trigger images of a lost time while his head spun. Thoughts of swimming suits and sun warmed girls, a friend's red TR-4 blaring "Satisfaction" and drinking beer by railroad tracks on a hushed summer night, all danced on the ceiling. He smiled. *Doug's sister is a nice girl,* he thought.

Lot looked at the marine positions on hill 881 south

through Trung Ly's binoculars. He had killed Trung Ly two days ago. The political officer had lost too much blood from his wound and had become a burden.

There was not enough food for both of them to survive and Lot had decided it was time to change sides again. He simply cut Ly's throat while he slept. Now he watched the marines and planned how best to approach them and surrender without being shot.

His stomach rumbled as he thought. He had eaten the last of the food two days ago. His first plan had been to return to his village, Lang Vei, and approach the American Special Forces soldiers he knew there. Then his family and friends would have time to escape before the North Vietnamese attacked.

He had started toward Lang Vei, but had spotted a North Vietnamese patrol and turned back to the mountains. It would not do for them to find him. There would be questions about what happened to the political officer and they would want him to lead them to the body. Besides they would never allow him to get his family out of the village before they attacked, he thought.

Lot hid his rifle and ammunition under some vines. It was time now. He would tell the Americans everything he knew about the North Vietnamese plans to attack. They would feed him well and move his people from the village.

He reached into his shirt pocket and pulled out a white piece of paper which had been folded many times into a small square. It was a surrender leaflet dropped by the Americans months ago around his village. He had kept it carefully hidden in his pack for just such an occasion.

He was in a small clearing 300 meters form the nearest Marine position. He would wait here for them to come and get him and lead him through the minefield blindfolded.

He smiled and stood up waving the piece of paper over his head. Chu Hoi!, Chu Hoi!, he yelled at the nearest Marine position.

Chapter Ten

The radio was still playing softly when he opened his eyes. Moonlight flickered across the shadow-filled room. O'Bryan sensed someone and looked up to see her form standing next to him. She's leaving, he thought and reached his right hand out to her. She took it and held it for a moment.

He pulled her closer to the bed and kissed her hand. She stood silent and motionless for a moment. He dropped her hand and sat up slowly in bed. She removed her white blouse cautiously, held it in front of her then dropped it to the floor.

He lay back on the bed and closed his eyes. He arched his back and slipped his slacks and underwear off. His eyes were still closed. He was wondering if this was another maddening dream. The only the sound was the low music and the rustle of her clothing falling away.

After a little while he opened his eyes, thinking it was a dream and that maybe she had gone, but she still stood next to him now wearing only panties. Then she knelt on the bed next to him, bent and kissed him softly on the lips, the chest, and down his brown flat stomach.

O'Bryan could see her clearly now in the moonlight from the window. Proud, taut breasts and a narrow waist that disappeared into the round curves of her hips. She's beautiful, he thought.

Susan Williams looked down at the young brown body on the crisp white sheets. She was breathing quickly and felt a little light-headed. She wondered if it was the vodka or excitement that caused her head to spin.

She had been aroused by the slow dancing with him, but the deep feelings of loss she had stored away had overwhelmed that. She had awakened, crept out of bed and been just about to leave when she stopped to look at him. How useless it would be for him to die, she had thought. Then he had reached for her hand and the idea came. Maybe she could stop just this one.

Damn this is crazy, she thought, but there was something slightly dangerous about this boy she hardly knew, which made it all the more exciting.

Still kneeling on the bed next to him, she placed one knee beside his hip, then swung the other leg over him, so that she straddled him now. She reached down and took him in her hand, then very slowly lowered herself down on him.

He stirred slightly then began to explore her soft roundness with his hands. He had forgotten how incredibly soft a woman's body felt.

The lovemaking was a slow exquisite variety which built until they were both consumed in an arching intertwined climax. She slumped forward on his chest.

In a moment she slid her legs from on top of his and moved to a place next to him, with her head on his chest and an arm around his waist. Soon she was asleep again.

O'Bryan gently brushed aside her fine brown hair which sprawled across his chest. He could barely believe this had happened, but it fit well into the unreality of his recent life. He watched her sleep and in a few minutes he inched out from under her and padded to the bathroom.

When he returned, he slipped a sheet over her and crept into the bed on the opposite side. He knew that he would never be able to sleep with someone touching him.

As he fell asleep looking across the bed at her, a line from the Beatles's "Norwegian Wood" raced across his mind and he smiled in the night *"I once had a girl or should I say she once had me."*

In the early dawn light he sensed movement. Through half-closed eyes he watched her scamper silently around the room collecting her clothing. She slipped into the bathroom and closed the door behind her. He heard running water and in a few minutes the bathroom door opened. She appeared from the darkened bathroom holding her shoes, and padded lightly to the door.

"Goodbye," he said, "in case I don't see you again."

She had her back to him and jumped, startled by his voice as she reached for the door. She twisted around. "No, not goodbye, see you later," she waved and went out the door.

He did not see or hear from her the next two days. He filled his days by going to movies, visiting bookstores and sleeping. He felt so tired all the time. It seemed to him that he could never get enough sleep. He thought he might be lonely and depressed, but he was just too tired to know or care.

Each day he felt stronger and a little more restless. He checked the hotel desk for messages from her but there was nothing. Finally, on Friday afternoon there was a message for him and a phone number.

His pulse quickened as he sat in the room and looked at the telephone. He made himself wait a full minute before he called her. She answered on the second ring.

"Hello?"

"Susan?" he asked.

"Well, Mr. O'Bryan, I thought maybe you went back to Oklahoma."

"No, been waiting to hear from you."

"I've called your room five times the last few days. Where have you been?"

"Why didn't you leave a message?"

"Well," she paused, "I kept thinking you would call. What have you been doing?"

"Not much, went to see a couple of movies, bought a tape recorder and some music, been reading a book."

"Sounds pretty exciting, kind of like hibernation. What are you reading?"

"*War and Peace.*"

She laughed. "Sounds like something you could get into."

"It's thick enough, should finish it by the time my extension is up in Vietnam."

"Are you really reading *War and Peace*?"

"Yep."

"I don't know about you. How about getting out of that hotel room. Are you up for a shopping trip?"

"Sure, I need to find something for my sister and get it in the mail."

"OK, I'll pick you up tomorrow morning in front of the hotel. Be ready, eight o'clock sharp, or what is it you marines say, zero eight hundred."

"Yes, ma'am," he said saluting the phone receiver, "zero eight hundred."

She giggled, "see you then," and hung up.

In the morning the weather was unseasonably warm,

even for southern California. He watched the news and weather on television and noted it was cold with a chance of snow in Oklahoma.

He dressed and withdrew some money from the hotel safe for Christmas shopping. He stood in front of the hotel waiting on her for fifteen minutes. Finally he spotted the red Corvair weaving its way through traffic. She wheeled to the curb and came to an abrupt halt next to him, in the red area marked passenger loading and unloading. She reached across and unlocked the door.

He was barely seated when the car accelerated and swerved into the downtown traffic congestion.

"Hi," she said and smiled a sideways glance at him.

"Hi, yourself," he replied bracing himself with a hand on the dash.

She wore a white U.C.L.A. sweat shirt and cut off jeans. Her white tennis shoes were a blur on the gas and clutch pedals as she speed-shifted the little car into and out of traffic lanes.

"How do you ever learn to get around in this traffic?"

"You learn," she replied without looking at him. "It's the quick and the dead out here, if you hesitate you never get anywhere."

"What have you been up to the last few days?" he asked, relaxing his grip on the dashboard.

"Working for the most part. I am doing a sort of internship at an ad agency. Might turn into a job when I graduate this spring."

They drove on in an awkward silence for a few miles until she spoke again. "You remember I told you there was a guy I was seeing, Tom Parkhurst?"

"Law student," commented O'Bryan looking ahead at

the traffic.

"Yes, well he has been in Sacramento visiting his parents. He came back last night and we went to dinner."

With considerable effort he didn't turn to look at her but knew she glanced sideways at him looking for his reaction. He sat dead still looking straight ahead. He had warned himself not to make too much of one night with her. After all, he thought, I did drop into her life with no notice.

"I told Tom about you." She hesitated. "I mean about you being in town and coming to my parents' for dinner."

O'Bryan now turned his head slowly and looked at her with a cold smile; her face was beginning to flush. "You should bring him by sometime, I'd like to meet him."

"I just bet you would, but unfortunately for you, he has gone back to Sacramento to be with his family for Christmas. He can't get back here until New Year's Eve."

O'Bryan leaned back in the bucket seat and folded his arms across his chest. He solemnly nodded his head sideways. "That's too bad, really tough luck."

This time she twisted her whole body to look at him with raised eyebrows. "You are evil, John O'Bryan. Don't expect what happened the other night to be an everyday occurrence. I really have never done anything like that before." The little car lurched into another lane to emphasize her words.

He grabbed the dash with both hands. "I don't expect anything from you, and watch where you're going, you're the one who brought all this up."

"Well, just so you understand, let's just be friends."

"That's fine with me," he said, sitting back again, then under his breath, "but it may be too late for friends."

She heard him but chose to ignore the comment. "Let's try, there's a great little shopping center up ahead, we can start there." She signaled and exited the freeway without another word.

O'Bryan followed her from store to store in the shopping center. At a jewelry store she helped him select a necklace for his sister. He had no idea what size clothing she wore now, so a necklace seemed a safe choice. It was gold with a small diamond-chipped heart. Susan assured him that his sister would love it.

He followed in her wake and carried packages, as she bought shirts, ties, wallets, and a beautiful white wool skirt for her mother. He noticed she paid for most of the gifts with credit cards. *Daddy does have money,* he thought.

All the stores were packed with Christmas shoppers who hurried with a sense of urgency and desperation, which he found oddly amusing. When he and Susan stopped for food in one of the shopping center restaurants, she noticed the little smile on his face.

"What's so funny?" she asked, taking a bite of her hamburger.

"Nothing really, it's just that all these people look so serious. In Vietnam we call America 'The World.' It is like a different world back here. It's like the war doesn't exist or it's an aberration, some kind of hole in reality where people just fall away. Or maybe all this," he made a sweeping gesture with his hand, "isn't real."

"Why can't they both be real?" she asked.

He thought for a moment then leaned across the table until he was close enough to whisper, "Because if they are both real then all of it, everything all of us are doing is pure insanity."

She reached across the table while looking straight into his eyes and pinched his arm.

"Feel that?"

"Yes," he replied placing his hand over hers.

"Good, now finish your hamburger, I have a few more things to buy."

He laughed and chomped down.

It was dark when they arrived back at his hotel. She pulled in front of the hotel where she had picked him up. They sat for a moment in the car.

"Thanks for coming by," he said.

She leaned across the seat and kissed him lightly on the lips. "I think I'll come over tomorrow and pick you up about nine. We can have breakfast at my place then wrap presents and get your sister's gift in the mail. Is that OK?"

"Sure," he said getting out of the car."

"See you then," she waved and pulled away into the traffic.

During the next few days they fell into a routine. She would pick him up in the mornings, when she wasn't working, and they would spend the day together. He had begun to feel completely at ease with her, as if they shared some sort of history. He even helped her clean her apartment. When they were finished she surveyed it.

"You know, O'Bryan, I think you're becoming domesticated."

He reached and put an arm around her waist. "Well I can be kept indoors, you know."

The phone rang and she crossed the room to answer it. He could tell now by the way she said "Hi," that it was Tom calling from Sacramento. To his annoyance, Tom called her every day.

He sat on the sofa and watched her as she talked. He really couldn't be angry with her. Tom was her future. Tom was a known quantity. O'Bryan knew he would leave soon, maybe to never return. He was too much of a risk for her to turn her life inside out.

He had Christmas dinner with her and her parents. It felt nice to him, being with a family for the holiday. It had been so long. But it was also the first Christmas for the family without Doug, an unspoken fact he felt hovering around the evening just beyond the tinsel and lights. Christmas night, after the dinner, instead of returning him to his hotel, she took him back to her apartment.

As he got out of the car he reached under the front seat for a present he had hidden there days ago. He panicked for a moment until he felt it. It had slipped to the very back of the seat, but it was still there.

He retrieved it and held it behind his back as he followed her up the steps to her apartment. Once inside, he sat quickly on the sofa with the gift still behind him, while she went into the kitchen. She returned with two mixed drinks.

"Merry Christmas," she said, offering one to him.

"Merry Christmas," he replied, holding out a red and white wrapped package to her."

She accepted the shoe box sized gift, sat down in a love seat opposite him and unwrapped the package on the coffee table.

"A cassette recorder and some tapes. Thank you."

"You're welcome. I bought one just like it for myself. I thought that maybe we could send some tapes back and forth. You know, hearing a voice is more like really talking to each other."

She sipped her drink and examined the recorder. He reached across the table and turned the recorder over.

"See, it's got a power cord and it runs on batteries too. I already put some batteries in there."

She turned the recorder back over. "What a great idea."

"Thank you, but it's not completely original. One of the officers I knew had the same setup. He would get tapes in the mail from his wife. I thought it was a good idea."

She sat the recorder down, finished her drink and stood up. "I got something for you too," she said, then walked off down the hallway.

"You really didn't need to," he said after her.

He sat sipping his drink and playing with the recorder. She had been gone about five minutes and he began to wonder what she was getting.

Suddenly one bare long leg snaked out from the darkness of the hall doorway. She leaned around the door frame and yelled "Catch."

He could see that she was wearing the same blue satin panties and sheer top that he remembered only too well from the first night they met. He dropped the recorder on the coffee table and caught the soft square green package which tumbled across the room.

"Careful," she yelled. "Merry Christmas."

He ripped away green ribbon and a bow, then peeled the paper away to find a pair of powder blue pajama shorts and pullover top. "Thanks," he said holding them up for inspection. "These beat the hell out of skivvies."

She stepped from the shadows of the hallway and stood facing him with her hands on her hips. "Are you going to sit out here all night with that machine, or are you going to turn out the lights and come to bed? You can put those on later."

He jumped from the divan and she turned and ran for the bedroom. He caught her just as she reached the bed and they landed on the mattress in a tangled heap.

This time the lovemaking was fast and hungry with no hint of sadness. There were laughs and giggles mixed with the moans of lust. When it was done they were both covered in a fine wet sheen and lay exhausted side by side. Finally when breathing returned to normal, she rolled to one elbow and looked at him in the semidarkness.

"God, I'm going to miss you," she sighed. "There is some sort of physical chemistry with us."

He rolled to an elbow to face her and reached to lift a stray lock of hair which fell across her face. When he was finished she continued.

"You know you don't have to go back there. I have some friends who can get you to Berkeley, then across the border to Canada. My friend's been there. He says there's a big farmhouse way out in the woods where you can stay. It's really isolated and safe."

"Thanks for the thought, but I don't think so."

"Why? Tell me why you think the war can't go on without you?"

"I'm afraid," he said softly, "it may be the other way around. Let's not waste time arguing about it. I only have a few days left."

"When is your flight back?"

"New Year's Day, six p.m."

They lay for a long time in the still, dark room, each one looking at the ceiling. Finally she broke the silence.

"Doug wouldn't have wanted you to go back if he were here."

He said nothing, but closed his eyes and thought, *I'm not sure he would want me here either.* He rose out of the rumpled bed and walked across the room.

"Where are you going?" she asked.

"To put on my Christmas present," he said over his shoulder.

"You come back here," she smiled. "I'll tell you when it's time to put them on."

In the morning he awakened and found her up, both dressed and coolly distant. She offered him breakfast but he wasn't hungry. He dressed and found her sitting in the living room holding her car keys.

"I have some errands to run, can I drop you at your hotel?"

"Sure," he said.

She drove him to the hotel's front entrance and pulled next to the curb. She turned and looked at him.

"I'll call you later."

He hesitated and turned as he got out of her car, making eye contact with her. He smiled. "That's what they all say."

She pulled quickly away from the curb. *Not even a kiss goodbye*, he thought, and walked inside.

He did not hear from her again until the day before News Year's Eve. He had spent the last few days wishing he had gone home to Washita instead of hanging around in L.A. If it had not been for her he would have gone home. Maybe some old friends would have been home for the holidays, but he had waited around, fascinated by her. He sat in his hotel bed, reading and pondering these thoughts

when the phone rang. He put down his paperback copy of
War and Peace and answered the phone.

"Hello?"

"Hi, how are you?" she asked.

"Bored and a little lonely, other than that, I'm fine."

"I'm sorry, but Tom's back in town and wants to go
out New Year's Eve."

"That's understandable," he replied.

"What time do you have to be at the airport tomorrow
night?"

"The plane leaves at six. I need to check in by 5:15.
Things are pretty hectic this time of year at airports."

"Listen, the reason I called is that I want to take you to
the airport."

"You don't have to do that, I understand."

Now there was a hint of anger in her voice. "Damn it,
O'Bryan, I want to see you again. I'll pick you up about
4:30. There are some things I need to say to you."

He dug a little deeper at her. "Are you sure it's not too
much trouble? What about Tom?"

"I'll worry about Tom. If you weren't so damn
stubborn there would be no questions about him. You
know that don't you?"

She waited for a reply but there was only silence.
Finally she said, "I'll see you tomorrow at 4:30."

"OK," he said, and she hung up.

He smiled at the receiver, then placed it back on the
cradle. *Strange girl*, he thought. He knew then that she
loved him. The fact that he was hopelessly in love with her
had to be pushed away from his considerations. He was
determined not to become the helpless victim of
unrequited love a second time. There were some things he

could not endure.

He fluffed up the pillows, decided to eat in the hotel restaurant and went back to *War and Peace.*

Los Angeles airport was packed with post-holiday crowds. Thousands of people trying to return to where they belonged. She walked quickly ahead of him then suddenly stopped. He turned to see her leaning against a white windowsill along the airport corridor.

The evening sunset filtered through the wide windows and created brilliant whites and deep blacks down the long corridor. He smiled and thought it oddly amusing that she had chosen a simple black dress for his going away. Her last protest at his insistence upon returning to the war.

She looked stunning in the dress, he thought. The sunlight from the window behind her struck her hair and framed her delicate face in auburn highlights. A smile curved the corners of her lips. She tilted her head a little to one side and looked up at him. "Last chance to change your mind."

"We talked this over and over. *You* know I can't."

She looked down. "I'd go with you," she said almost in a whisper.

He thought about it for a moment, caught by surprise by this new offer. She would walk away from everything for him. He could stay lost with her for a long time. The government really wouldn't look that hard for him. Maybe someday they could come back when the war was over.

He stood considering his future, gazing down at her. If he went with her he would always know inside that he didn't belong because of who he was and where he should be. He would lose the respect he had earned for himself and resent her for her part in that. They would be haunted by that and it would be no good. His silence was her answer. "I can't compete with her," she shouted, and raised her hands in mock surrender.

"Who are you talking about?"

"Your mother, your giant green mother!"

He laughed. "They usually stick another word on the end of mother if you're talking about the Marine Corps."

He looked at her with exaggerated surprise. "I don't talk about your family like that, do I?"

"God help us," she mumbled, then smiled and stepped close to him. He put his arms around her and breathed her perfumed warmth as he held her snug against him.

There was a certain desperation in the kiss, which betrayed her. The melancholy of seeing her for the last time combined with the exquisite joy of holding her made him lightheaded. He knew this moment must last him. It was all that he might ever have of her. It was as if he were a third party memorizing each detail as she unfolded in his arms. He looked down and saw silent tears. Her face began to flush.

"I'll write," he heard himself say.

She pulled her arms from around his waist and reached up to encircle his neck. Then, on tiptoes she pulled her mouth to his ear. "Damn you, O'Bryan." She mouthed the words softly, "If you get on that plane I don't ever want to see you again."

He stepped back and looked at her, unable to speak. He picked up his carry-on bag and turned away.

She watched his back disappear down the corridor to the boarding area. She expected him to stop or look back, but he just kept walking. She started to shout at him but the words caught in her throat. Thoughts of her brother's funeral flickered through her mind. Her own instinct for survival took over and she turned and walked away.

O'Bryan knew that if he paused or looked back he would never get on the plane. He shuffled in line onto the plane. His shoulders slumped and he felt ancient. He found an empty seat, sat down and buckled his seat belt. He leaned back and closed his eyes, exhausted.

Susan walked quickly through the airport lobby. Her knees felt weak and she sat down for a moment. She felt numb and hollow. She wondered if she would ever feel anything again.

Later, on the drive home, she turned on the car radio and heard the tail end of a news report. A reporter gave the casualty figures from a battle in the Central Highlands. She counted her own losses as the sun sank in the Pacific. *One dead, one missing and I'm a walking wounded,* she thought, and rocked slightly back and forth in the driver's seat.

As she drove, a fine California mist fell on the little Corvair and she was forced to turn on the windshield wipers. It soon turned into a steady drizzle.

Outside the base at Khe Sanh a hazy light began to show over the mountains. Vinh Nguyen crawled from a hole in the side of a hill and stood to stretch and await the sunrise. He was cold and stiff in the morning fog. Below, he could see morning fires glowing around the Marine airstrip on the plateau. He wished that he could make a fire, but took comfort in the knowledge that in three days' time the Americans would not dare light a fire.

Without a sound, other dark figures began to emerge in the fog on the hillside around him. They were 40,000 strong now and soon they would all be in place. He squatted down to unwrap a cold ball of rice. He said a silent prayer and knew that his father was watching this scene from somewhere and felt proud.

CHAPTER ELEVEN

During the return flight to Vietnam, O'Bryan slept most of the time, dozing off while reading his paperback book. Even though he knew the 707 was flying straight and level at 25,000 feet he could not escape the sensation of falling.

He reasoned with himself that it was because the return trip was much faster than the trip home had been. There was no layover in Okinawa, only a short refueling stop where more replacement troops were picked up. On the final leg of the flight, O'Bryan found himself surrounded by F.N.G.s, ("fucking new guys"), who sat wide-eyed and talked nervously with no idea of what was coming at them. He tried to ignore them and closed his eyes for the final plunge. He was falling further and faster and now, until the plane landed with a jolt on a runway at Da Nang.

He walked off the plane and the warm moist air, carrying the smell of aviation fuel along with the roar of Phantom jet engines, slammed into him. Something clicked inside his head and he was back.

An Air Force sergeant led them to the terminal building where he picked up his seabag from a cart which had just arrived from the plane's baggage compartment. Next they walked across the airstrip to the transit facility, which consisted of rows of long wooden huts.

As he stood in line with his travel orders waiting to check in he saw the silver 707 lift from the runway and climb steeply to avoid any would be V.C. snipers. He knew the civilian airliners were serviced and refueled with amazing speed without any of the crew ever setting foot on the soil. It added to the sense he felt of social quarantine that was imposed on anything which had contact with the war. He remembered that even the clean jungle utilities and boots he wore on the trip back had been confiscated and burned in Okinawa. He thought to himself, we are all disposable.

"Where you going?" the air force clerk asked, jerking him back to reality.

"Khe Sanh," answered O'Bryan, "First Battalion, Twenty-Sixth Marines.

Without looking up, the clerk spoke, "Be here tomorrow morning at 0800. Got a flight of ammunition and medical supplies going in on a C-130. Lots of shit going to Khe Sanh. Next."

"I'll be here," O'Bryan answered and turned away to find his billet.

The next morning he showered, shaved and ate breakfast in what he knew would soon be considered the luxury of the transit facility. He checked in at 0800 and had his name added to the flight manifest. The big green plane's belly was stacked full of pallets marked "ammunition" and "medical supplies." All of this was loaded in the middle of the plane's cargo bay on a bed of rollers, so that when the plane's rear ramp was lowered the cargo would be disgorged instantly on the runway. There was a small aisle left on either side of the cargo with just enough room for a person to squeeze down the length of the plane.

O'Bryan stood with his seabag at the rear of the plane with three other marines who looked like replacements, a Private and two P.F.C.'s. All three of them had a look of shock and bewilderment that was commonly found on faces new to the war. *More F.N.G.'s*, he thought.

The crew chief, who was an Air Force sergeant, waved them on board and O'Bryan hefted his seabag to his shoulder, then threaded his way down the narrow passage to the front of the cargo bay.

The chief stopped and released four aluminum frame jump seats from the side of the plane's fuselage, then bent and locked them into position. He stood and pointed, indicating that they should sit. The Air Force staff sergeant leaned against the bulkhead looking at his four passengers for a moment before beginning his preflight litany. "There's a seat belt strap for each seat," he began, bending to pull a loose strap from behind O'Bryan. "Strap yourselves in."

When this was done he went down the narrow row checking each man's seat belt and pulling them tight. "Anybody ever make an assault landing in a C-130?"

There was no response.

"OK, well what happens is we come in high and feather two of the engines. Then we make a steep dive on the runway, leveling out just before we touch down. We been getting some ground fire from the mountains around Khe Sanh when we make our approach, so this way we'll be a little harder to hit.

O'Bryan always found it endearing that the Air Force explained why they were about to do something. The Marine Corps never told why they were about to do anything. They just did it and when all hell broke loose, you just hoped there was a good reason for it.

The crew chief continued his speech. "When we touch down we will reverse the props and taxi to the turn around at the end of the runway. At that time the ramp will lower and we drop the cargo out the rear of the airplane. As soon as you see the cargo sliding down the rollers, you guys haul ass out the end of the ramp. Do not, repeat, do not go out a side exit. The propellers might make hamburger out of ya. The airplane ain't gonna stop for nothin'. So if you hesitate for any reason, it's a round trip. Got it? Any questions?"

O'Bryan shook his head no. The other three just sat and stared ahead silently.

"Here we go then, non-stop, Da Nang to Khe Sanh," yelled the crew chief. He smiled at his own little joke, walked to his station, plugged in his headset, and fastened a safety belt around his waist. The big plane's four engines increased pitch to a deafening roar, then the lumbering aircraft lurched forward, bumped down the runway and lifted off.

O'Bryan glanced over his left shoulder and saw the three F.N.G.'s sitting rigidly as if at attention, eyes wide in disbelief. Maybe, he thought, it was good to not tell grunts. It gave them too much time to think about it.

He wrapped his hand tightly through the strap on his seabag, which sat in front of him between his knees, then leaned back against the metal fuselage.

He closed his eyes and relaxed. The rumble and vibrations of the C-130's engines served as a soothing lullaby. He smiled. The new men would learn to rest anytime, anywhere they had a chance.

It seemed he had just drifted off to sleep when the image of Susan Williams, wearing her black airport dress floated to the surface of his subconscious. She smiled her little "I surrender" smile and then suddenly began to fall away. He felt himself falling away also and he reached for her but she receded into the blackness of space.

Nguyen and three new members of his Scout Forward Observer team sat in perfectly camouflaged spider holes, halfway up Hill 1015, overlooking the Khe Sanh Combat Base. The top of 1015 was occupied by a small group of marines, manning a radio relay station. Nguyen and his men had observed them being resupplied by helicopter. For this reason he and his men stayed hidden in their holes during the day, even in this dense undergrowth. Detection meant sure death; there were no helicopters to come for them.

At night, each of them took turns making an arduous trip of three miles up and down the mountain to a spot where they had concealed supplies of food and water. At the end of two weeks another four-man team would relieve them. This duty meant tedious hours confined in the narrow spider holes on clear days, but also offered a splendid panoramic view of Marine positions. Today was one of those clear days.

Nguyen's proficiency with a map and compass had marked him as one of the men for this job. He sat now with only his binoculars protruding from under the woven-bush cover of his one-man hole. In the week he had been here, he had pinpointed, with compass resections, each Marine artillery and ammunition position on the base.

Each man in his group was picked because he had a specialty. One was a skilled sniper, equipped with a

Russian-made sniper rifle and scope. The other two men had carried a 60mm mortar tube and baseplate with them. Their job was to fire at planes landing on the airstrip below, if they were afforded the opportunity. Nguyen had already taken three different azimuth readings on the middle and both ends of the air strip, and set out crude aiming stakes for the mortar crew.

The airstrip was located at nearly the maximum effective range of the little mortar, but it was in direct line of sight, which made adjustments easy. If they were lucky enough to hit a moving plane on the runway, the wreckage might severely restrict the American resupply effort.

He was surprised that he did not hear the cargo plane until it was nearly overhead. Quickly, he crawled to the holes where the mortar team dozed and awakened them. In a few minutes the mortar was assembled, barrel to baseplate, with one of the men using his shirt as a makeshift bipod. The barrel was lowered for maximum range and a four-round salvo lay ready on the ground next to them. After firing they would have to move immediately because the Americans would pulverize their position with artillery and possibly an air strike. Nguyen could think of no worse way to die than the sticky napalm flame. But it was worth it if they could hit the plane.

He lifted his binoculars and saw the C-130 in the sky above, diving steeply on the airstrip. It would be, he knew, a matter of timing and then some luck to hit the moving target. They waited motionless for the plane to touch down.

*   *   *

O'Bryan awakened with a fluttering feeling in his stomach and realized that he really was falling, along with the plane and all its cargo. The assault dive inside the C-130 felt just like a roller coaster ride he had taken once on a class trip to Oklahoma City. The bottom just dropped out of the world and for a moment, you were weightless as the plunge began. He and the other marines grabbed franticly at their seabags as they continued to fall.

The airplane finally nosed up and came back to level flight just before a jolt hit them and they were slammed backwards as it landed and reversed the huge propellers on the runway matting at Khe Sanh.

The crew chief unstrapped, jumped up, and signaled them to do the same. The plane taxied to the end of the runway and turned around. The rear ramp dropped and the big craft began to gain some speed back up the runway for takeoff. The crew chief released the safety straps and the cargo sleds began to roll out the back of the plane.

O'Bryan watched the cargo roll away down the ramp and waited for the other three passengers to move, but they stood frozen. He yelled at them and then, dragging his seabag, pushed by them down the plane's cargo ramp. He pushed his seabag out first, then jumped to the left side of the plane. Stumbling he cut his knees and both hands on the corrugated runway matting.

He sat on the runway examining his hands and knees when he heard the blast of the airplane's jet assist rocket packs fire. He looked up to see the plane climbing at an incredibly steep angle off the end of the runway. Puffs of gray smoke popped up where the plane had been on the runway and he heard someone yell, "Incoming, get the fuck off the runway!"

The warning wasn't needed. O'Bryan was already running at full speed with his seabag over his shoulder towards the yelling figure. When he reached the man, they both dropped into a small trench line that ran parallel to the runway. O'Bryan sat for a few minutes catching his breath and trying to orientate himself as more mortar fire impacted on the runway. The man sitting in the trench next to him had the words "Can Do" written on the side of his helmet. O'Bryan lit up a cigarette and inhaled deeply. "Seabee?" he asked offering his pack to his new acquaintance.

"Yeah," replied the Seabee, holding up his hand at the offered cigarettes "got a chew," and spat in the dirt next to them. "You hit?"

"No," said O'Bryan looking down at the blood on his hands. "Cut 'em on the runway matting."

"You only been here about five minutes and you already got a purple heart."

"Bullshit," answered O'Bryan, "Don't need one of those things, just means you screwed up. I been here before. Just got back from a thirty-day leave."

"You extended?"

"Yep."

"Well you fucked up comin' back here, they say we're surrounded, shit's about to hit the fan."

"I heard that before," O'Bryan replied, taking another deep drag and flinching as a nearby 105 howitzer battery fired a six-round salvo at the mortar position on the slope of hill 1015.

The Seabee stood up in the chest-high trench. Looking slowly in a half-circle, he spat again. "Guess the fireworks are over, plane's gone."

O'Bryan also stood and brushed the red dirt from his clothes. "They shoot at every plane that comes in here now?" he asked.

The Seabee smiled, exposing tobacco and teeth. "Only the ones that land. I better haul my ass up there and get the fork lift runin'."

O'Bryan watched as the man calmly walked to an eight-foot pile of sandbags, which concealed a fork lift. He drove the fork lift on to the runway and began removing pallets laden with supplies.

He looked around, still standing in the trench.

Things had changed while he was gone. There were fresh trenches and bunkers in every direction. He pulled himself out of the trench and started down the reddish brown dirt road for First Battalion Headquarters.

He found Battalion Headquarters in a small green wooden hut where he had remembered it thirty days ago. Next to the hut a six-man working party was methodically digging a bunker large enough to hold the headquarters' staff. After reporting in and having his orders stamped he went to his company command post.

Captain Hudson sat behind a folding desk flanked by two clerks. He stood and shook O'Bryan's hand. "Glad to see you back, O'Bryan, how was the leave?"

"Just fine, sir."

"You got back just in time. We lost a Forward Observer Team last week on a patrol and there's not going to be any replacements for them for a while. How would you like to be an F.O. for the Company?"

O'Bryan thought for a little before answering. "I don't know, sir. I really don't have any formal training. I was a volunteer radio operator for an F.O. for two months, but I never really was an F.O.."

"You know how to read a map, don't you?"

"Yes, sir."

"You know fire mission procedure for artillery and mortars, don't you?"

"Yes, sir."

"O.J.T. will have to do. You are now officially my Forward Observer. I'll see that you're issued a map of the area and a compass."

O'Bryan knew that it was futile to argue his lack of training. The assignment had been made. He simply answered again, "Yes, sir, I'll do the best I can."

"The next decent replacement that comes in will be your radio man. For now, you carry your own radio." The Captain paused and reached for a sheet of paper in a file folder. He handed O'Bryan the paper and said, "Is all that clear, Corporal?"

O'Bryan looked down and saw that what the Captain had handed him was a warrant promoting one John D. O'Bryan to the rank of Corporal. He was shocked. Most of the Corporals he knew had completed at least one four-year enlistment.

The Captain smiled. "This came through while you were on leave, congratulations."

"Thank you, sir," muttered O'Bryan, still staring down at the warrant.

"Report to Lt. Henderson on the south end of the perimeter, after you draw your weapon and 782 gear. Tell him that you'll billet with his platoon but you're assigned to me until further notice as an F.O. Study those maps and brush up on your fire procedure. I'll have a radio sent out to you. I think you're going to have plenty of fire mission targets to shoot at."

"That's what I hear, sir. What's the word?"

"The word is that an N.V.A. gave himself up to a company on 881 South. Claims the N.V.A. are building up strength for something big. Probably try to overrun the base. Come at us in Division strength with artillery support and maybe tanks."

O'Bryan blurted, "Tanks?"

The Captain continued, ignoring the interruption, "As you noticed, we have beefed up some too, and there's more help on the way."

"I noticed the place seemed pretty crowded."

"A reinforced regiment of our own artillery and a few tanks."

"How many N.V.A. you figure are out there, Skipper?" O'Bryan asked in a low voice, looking over his shoulder to the doorway.

The Captain paused, then answered in an equally low tone. "Intelligence figures between ten and twenty thousand. Keep that figure to yourself. Just get ready."

"Yes, sir, and thank you." O'Bryan turned to go draw his gear. He walked along the road that circled the inside of the base to reach the supply tent. He was elated at making Corporal, and flattered that the skipper had entrusted him with some intelligence facts. But as he digested what the Captain said, he decided that it wouldn't make much difference if he died as an E-3 or E-4.

Next to the supply tent was a huge metal shipping container called a conex (metal shipping) box. It was half buried in a hole twenty feet wide by twenty feet deep. Marines were busy filling sandbags, which they stacked on the top while others transferred supplies to the container.

Everywhere he looked marines were digging, moving underground. As usual, he thought, the word was already out. After drawing his gear, he reported to Lt. Henderson, who was glad to see him, but disappointed he wasn't going to be a squad leader in his platoon. He moved into the bunker that had been occupied by the two-man F.O. team that he was replacing.

Days rolled into weeks as his life began to assume routines again. In the mornings he dug deeper in the bunker, which the other two men had started, and filled more sandbags, which he stacked along the bunker's sides.

He gradually doubled the thickness of the outside walls and even managed to scrounge a sheet of runway matting from the Seabee he had met. He stacked rows of red dirt-filled sandbags on the steel matting for the bunker's roof.

In the afternoon he studied a map of the Khe Sanh area, using his compass to plot resections from known terrain features. He called in practice fire missions to artillery and mortar units until he was satisfied that he was proficient.

The standard of living had risen at Khe Sanh during his absence. With the additional troops had come some benefits such as hot chow and even an occasional outdoor movie.

He did not care to meet the new men. Since his return, the few men left who had been his friends were going home. As each of them departed they would come by his bunker and give him their remaining candles and C-rations as going away gifts. They never said much, just "Thought you might want this shit man," or "Keep your ass down," but he understood the looks they gave him. They all knew what was coming and they were escaping.

After dark, he sat alone in his bunker, read *War and Peace* by candlelight, and waited.

Nguyen and his men moved slowly, single file through the elephant grass along the valley floor in the starless night. It had taken his team two weeks, moving exclusively at night by compass in a wide arch around the base, to reach the foot of the Co Roc mountains across the Laotian border. There, he would deliver his hand-drawn maps of the Marine positions at Khe Sanh to his regimental commander and receive his next assignment.

Walking in the cool security of night, he reflected on the letter he had posted two months ago to Thi in Hanoi. Summoning all his courage, he had written her and proposed marriage. Her commanding officer would have to approve, but that was rarely a problem.

He had told her that although he had spent only a short time with her, he felt as if they had always known each other. He confessed to her that his love for her was the spiritual food which nourished him through all the war's hardships, and he thought of her constantly. Should he have told her that? Maybe he was too bold and would frighten her.

A tingle ran down his spine as he reached and parted the elephant grass in front of him. If he accomplished nothing else before his life ended, at least he had told her the truth. His love for her had made it all meaningful. Her reply should be there when he reached the Co Roc camp. He quickened his pace toward the mountains.

Nguyen's team gasped for air and struggled to keep up

with him. After three hours at a grueling uphill pace, they halted to await the dawn. Soon they would encounter outposts of his regiment and Nguyen wanted to be certain there were no mistaken identity accidents. A gentle mountain breeze cooled their sweat-drenched bodies as a light haze outlined the mountains facing them in silence.

Nguyen's heart pounded.

By 10 a.m. he and his team had reached the mountain bunker of the Regimental Commander. Nguyen dismissed his team to find food and prepare a place to rest. He reported to Colonel Linh and presented his maps of the Marine base. Linh was a short, stocky, and seemingly tireless man whom Nguyen had great respect for.

"Lieutenant," Linh said looking up from the maps spread on a wooden crate table, "you have done a wonderful service for our cause. We will concentrate our first barrages on the American strong points and ammunition caches you have marked. Go and congratulate your men, then rest. Tonight we move in for the attack and we will need you to direct our fire."

"Thank you, sir," Nguyen replied. "If you have any questions about the markings on the maps, I will be with the political officer collecting our mail. Also sir, has there been any news of the political officer Trung Ly or the mountain villager Lot?"

"No, we must assume they are dead, lost or captured."

"Yes, sir, but I am afraid Lot would betray us to the Americans given the chance to do so."

"It's too late to worry about such things now, Lieutenant. Now go and rest.

"Yes, sir."

The letter from Thi was waiting for him. He could

barely contain himself at the sight of her small, neat handwriting on the envelope. He noticed that all the mail had been opened and the political officer smiled at him as he handed him the mail.

Nguyen exercised his iron discipline and made himself wait until he had delivered his men's mail to open his own. He found a quiet place behind some large rocks, folded his legs beneath him and began to read:

My Dearest,

I received your letter and I accept your proposal of marriage. I had to wait three days for my commander to return to ask for his permission. Please forgive me, as I know you must be anxious for my reply, but loving you means that I must think about our future and what it might hold. As you know, I have taken an oath of responsibility to the motherland. I must be ready to serve or take part in combat until the war is done. President Ho has declared that we should go on fighting for another five, ten, or even twenty years. From our generation to the next if need be. My love, we can not marry yet! We both still have much yet to do. But I do love you. Sometime in the future we will be united as our country will be. Until then, I will wait faithfully for you to return and our day of victory.

Be patient my love.

Yours Always,
Thi

Nguyen's chin dropped to his chest. He was at once joyous and miserable. He longed to hold her, shake her, and speak to her face-to-face. He folded the letter carefully and placed it with her photo inside the plastic bag where he kept it hidden.

He leaned back against the rock, now suddenly fatigued. *Didn't Thi understand?* he thought. Unless they and others like them married soon, there would be no next generation to fight President Ho's precious war. He began to doubt that they would ever see each other again.

O'Bryan settled down in his bunker for the night. He checked his rubber lady and found it had lost a little air during the day. He blew the air mattress back to capacity, removed his boots and lay down, spreading his poncho liner over himself. The bunker was damp, musty and dark.

Mail had come today, but there was nothing for him. He had hoped that Susan might write him a note but he knew she wouldn't. It was best that she got on with her life and he resumed his. Maybe, he thought, once he was home for good he would call her. She would probably be married by then. How would she feel about adultery? He laughed out loud at his own mental rambling. The last thing he pondered before sleep was how many men were in an N.V.A. division.

The shockwave of the blast reached him before the screams of other marines. It blew the poncho liner off him as his eyes opened and he spat falling dirt from the roof. White light from a towering fireball, made by the detonation of 1500 tons of high explosives rising from the ammo dump 200 yards away blinded him.

He curled into a ball hugging his knees to his chest. After a few minutes he sat up. It had started, he thought and soon a massive ground attack would follow the shelling. He quickly pulled on his jungle boots, cursing himself for taking them off. Throwing on his flak jacket, he grabbed his helmet and rifle then ran out of his bunker into a six-foot connecting trench.

The off-key whistle of point detonating artillery rounds tumbling end over end caused him to immediately flatten in the trench as shells continued to rain down in a massive chain reaction. After crawling a few feet on his hands and knees he heard an explosion from above and to his left. Hot jagged metal showered around him. He could see the squad bunker down the trench line was still intact. It was impossible to stay outside, he reasoned. Anything above ground would be shredded by shrapnel and with airbursts above, not even the trench afforded cover.

I'm the only dumb son of bitch out here, he thought and ran bent low in the trench back to the relative safety of his own bunker. Once inside he removed his helmet and took two cigarettes from a package, pulled the filters of the ends and placed the filters in his ears. He hoped his ear drums weren't already ruptured.

The cigarette ear plugs helped some. He put his helmet back on and sat by the bunker entrance searching the flash-lit night for attacking N.V.A. Another giant explosion from the direction of the ammo dump rocked his bunker and sent him rolling backwards.

He crawled deeper into the blackness of his bunker and laughed out loud. *What am I worried about,* he thought. The North Vietnamese would all die from their own secondary explosions if they assaulted. As long as the ammunition continued to explode no one could move above the ground. He sat his rifle next to him and stared out the bunker entrance.

The blasts were oddly comforting to him now. The scene reminded him of lightning storms on the Oklahoma plains as, for frozen split seconds, they revealed the carnage outside. In one of those flashing split seconds he saw something beyond belief.

Silhouetted by explosions was the outline of a bulldozer atop an earthen berm at the ammo dump, pushing dirt over the piles of exploding burning ammunition. O'Bryan thought of the Seabee who had greeted him at the runway and later had given him the corrugated steel matting for his roof. He didn't know the man's name, but no matter, if he survived, O'Bryan knew he would recognize him. He would be the man with the biggest set of balls at Khe Sanh. The N.V.A. gunners continued to pour in 122mm rocket fire. He lit one of his now filterless cigarettes and smiled. What a show he thought.

A thousand meters away Nguyen watched from a freshly dug trench as huge fireballs erupted over the Marine base. How could anyone survive that he thought. According to the plan when the bombardment slackened, he was to lead a company to the west side of the base perimeter and probe the Marine positions in preparation for the main attack. Of course it was impossible to carry out any sort of attack now. They would have to wait for the explosions to stop. He wondered how long would that be. This would upset the timing as the assaults on the hills north of the base were to coincide with the main assault.

War never went as planned, he knew that as fact. Many of the men around him joked that it was only a matter of time now. The Americans were all blowing up from their own ammunition. Nguyen did not joke. He knew that this was only a delay they could not afford. Soon the weather would be clear and the sky would be filled with American planes. Surprise was wasted now. This would be a long fight.

CHAPTER TWELVE

The main ammunition dump continued to explode through the night and into the morning of the next day. By the next afternoon the ammunition cook offs had become infrequent enough that O'Bryan and the other marines felt safe to come out of their bunkers and make full-speed dashes from point to point above ground.

Corpsmen and stretcher bearers scurried about collecting the wounded and running them to a large underground aid station dubbed "Charlie Med" on the north end of the base. The dead lay wrapped in green poncho shrouds awaiting rubber body bags and a trip to the grave's registration shed.

Most of the men stayed in the safety of the trench lines, peeking over the top to survey the damage. What few structures there were remaining above ground, were the targets of continued rocket and mortar barrages which slammed into the base with alarming regularity. O'Bryan visited the men in the squad bunker and found them all alive but dazed. The grunts staggered around with a vacant look in their eyes, the result of little sleep and too much high explosives.

The sun came and went without much notice behind a gray gauze of clouds, which prevented any immediate air strikes. North Vietnamese snipers took advantage of this opportunity and set up along the slopes of the surrounding hills, picking off some of the careless or dazed marines.

A daily routine began to emerge for O'Bryan and the others living in the rubble. Each morning at dawn, when the fog reduced visibility to a few feet, N.V.A. gunners would open fire with a 75mm recoilless rifle. They fired blindly into the base with no particular target in mind. Sometimes they scored direct hits on bunkers killing or maiming marines in their sleep and other times the rounds exploded harmlessly in a vacant area. The grunts dubbed this the reckless rifle and used it as a sort of crude alarm clock that went off every morning.

O'Bryan noticed that like the impact of the reckless rifle, death had become a random event inside Khe Sanh. On the fourth day of the attack Corporal Johnson was killed. A sniper shot Johnson on his way to draw C-rations for his squad.

O'Bryan took over Johnson's squad which was housed conveniently in a bunker just around a bend in the trench line. O'Bryan opted to stay in his present digs believing that it might be bad luck to move into a dead man's spot.

Because of casualties, there were now bunkers that were unoccupied. Now, if incoming rockets landed too close to an occupied bunker, men simply picked up all their gear and moved to a vacant hole in the ground. O'Bryan was amused watching the daily migration of superstitious grunts. He thought of this whole process and dubbed it "bunker roulette." Some men tried to move every other day hoping to beat the odds. It was all very spooky to watch he thought.

This morning Lt. Henderson sipped coffee from a C-ration can and watched from atop his bunker while his men played the morning session of "bunker roulette." He grew impatient as several groups clustered around prime vacant housing. "You people spread out. Don't want one rocket round wipein' out a whole squad." The men began to disperse down the trench line. Henderson called after them. "Pass the word, squad leaders to my bunker." The word echoed in the fog down the Marine trench, "Squad leaders to the C.P."

When all four squad leaders were assembled sitting on the bunker's dirt floor, Lt. Henderson, enthroned on two wooden ammo crates began. "We had a briefing this morning. The skipper says that the N.V.A. tried to overrun 881 but got caught in the wire. They will hit us soon with everything they got. Soon as they can get ten or twelve thousand of 'em together in one spot. No one is comin' to help us. When the weather clears we got all the air support they can give us. Tell your people to stay low tonight. B-52s are gonna blow the shit out of everything up to 500 meters from our wire. We will probably catch some hot shrapnel from that."

O'Bryan whistled his concern. The lieutenant looked down for a moment then gravely continued his briefing.

"There are also some instructions to pass on to the men about what to do if we are overrun."

"Oh shit," O'Bryan mumbled in unison with the other three squad leaders.

Henderson continued trying to reassure his leaders. "No one is sayin' we will be overrun, but you always need to prepare for the worst. So this is the plan. If the N.V.A. penetrate and overrun our positions, tell your men to try to hide under the dead bodies in the trenches. There should be plenty of those around if things come to that stage in an all out attack. After the N.V.A. pass over the trench, then whoever is left alive should raise up and attack them from behind. Kill as many as you can. Then try to filter out through the wire. If you can't do that then find the best cover you can and stay down. After that, whoever is senior should organize pockets of resistance and wait for help. Any questions?"

The four squad leaders sat in stunned silence digesting this latest morsel of information from on high. Finally, O'Bryan broke the silence.

"Mr. Henderson, I don't think this is a very good plan, seein' as how we nearly all end up dead in this plan."

"I agree," Henderson replied curtly. "Let's hope we never have to use it."

O'Bryan shook his head. "My squad is already spooked, Lieutenant. You sure you want us to pass this on to them?"

"I don't like it either," the Lieutenant said rising to a bent six foot, three inches in the low bunker, "but that's the word so pass it on. Any more questions?"

A silence as thick as the morning fog filled the bunker.

"OK, that's it. Keep your squads busy. I want weapons cleaned and inspected daily. Repair any damage to bunkers or trench works. That's all for now."

The squad leaders filed out of Henderson's bunker one at a time, disappearing to spread the word. O'Bryan hesitated at the narrow opening that served as the doorway. He had waited until it was just he and the lieutenant. He wanted to take this opportunity, before the lieutenant's ever present radio operator returned. He turned to face his Platoon Commander.

"Mr. Henderson, I do have just one more question. I have been over here long enough to know that if we get overrun, 6000 marines, shit will hit the fan from Saigon to Washington D.C. A lot of people's careers go down the tubes, maybe from the President on down. Lots of people are gonna fall on their swords. What I mean, Lieutenant, if we get overrun they are gonna call in thousand-pound bombs or B-52s all over this place. Anyone who survives the attack will probably get killed in the air strikes afterward. Isn't that right?"

Henderson arched one eyebrow. He looked at O'Bryan with a renewed respect. "You are absolutely right, Corporal. But keep that to yourself. Why do you think I threw that little part in about filtering through the wire if you were lucky enough to survive all that shit. That wasn't in the briefing. We are all expected to die like good marines though. Personally, I expect to be dead long before air strikes become a worry. You know all grunts are sooner or later expendable."

"I know that, Lieutenant, I've seen enough of 'em die. I just like to know what the odds are all the time. Even when worst comes to worst. You never know, even the Alamo had a couple of survivors."

"You from Texas, O'Bryan?"

"Hell no, sir. That's an insult. I'm from Oklahoma."

O'Bryan smiled broadly, showing white teeth against his red clay stained face. "I just watched every episode of Davey Crockett on Walt Disney, Sunday evenings."

The lieutenant returned O'Bryan's grin. "Well this isn't the Alamo yet, and you ain't Davey Crockett, so get back and get your squad to work."

"Yes, sir," O'Bryan answered, turning to leave the bunker. He now knew the whole truth about what the worst could be.

CHAPTER THIRTEEN

O'Bryan called for a squad meeting in his bunker. He put Renarie in charge of rounding up everyone. There were fourteen men in O'Bryan's squad, counting O'Bryan himself. They were short one man, Rankin, who was wounded that morning. So, that left them thirteen strong, which everyone considered an unlucky number. The men squatted shoulder to shoulder in the shadows of the dark musty hole. Some leaned in around the bunker entrance. Renarie spoke up, "When we goin' to get a replacement for Rankin?" O'Bryan peered in the semidarkness at Renarie. "Jesus, Renarie, he just got shot this morning. Soon as another plane comes in with re-supply stuff, we might get somebody."

"Well," Renarie stammered, "It's just that we don't like havin' thirteen guys. You know. It's bad luck. We don't need no fuckin' bad luck."

O'Bryan considered this for a moment. "I want you guys to forget about that luck shit. If you want to think about crap like that, then think about this. I've been here damned near longer than anyone in the regiment, and I ain't never been hit. So, I must be good luck, and bein' in my squad is good luck all by itself. It cancels out any of that thirteen shit."

Renarie and the rest of the men considered the logic of this for a moment and then grunted their individual expressions of approval. O'Bryan then explained the plan, given to him by Lt. Henderson, for all of them if the base was overrun.

When O'Bryan had finished, Ranarie again spoke up,

"That's the worst fuckin' plan I ever heard of. Who thought that up, some dipshit in Saigon?"

O'Bryan agreed, "I know! I know! It's a fucked up plan. If things get to that point around here, you have my permission to do whatever you want to do, Renarie, cause it really won't fuckin' matter much."

"The rest of you guys stay with me cause I've got the luck...now on to more important shit. We are going to build a new squad bunker." This drew several "ah shit"s and "fuck"s from the assembled squad.

The idea had come to O'Bryan during the long hours while the ammunition dump exploded. It would be a way to keep the men busy and might actually do some good.

O'Bryan continued, "Not just a bunker, but the perfect bunker that can withstand a direct hit from an 82mm mortar round and maybe even a 122mm rocket."

Questions came fast:

"Where we gonna get the shit to build it with?"

"What about sniper fire?"

"How deep should it be?"

"How many layers of sandbags does it take to stop an 82mm mortar round?

O'Bryan held up a hand in the semidarkness.

"Don't worry. Don't worry. I thought about all that stuff. I got a buddy in the C.B.s that will help us scrounge up the material we need including steel runway matting sections. I'm telling you this will be the envy of the whole company. When we get this thing dug and finished, we can sit in comfort and safety while the gooks pour in the incoming! We start first thing tomorrow morning. Fire team leaders, make up your watch lists and draw your C-rations for tonight and breakfast. Remember, water is only for drinking, no shavin' or washin' till you get the word...any questions?"

A hand shot up. It was P.F.C. Borden, a short blond-headed kid from Chicago, otherwise known to the squad as the "little fuck" because of his theft of numerous cans of C-ration peaches and pound cake. Borden would remove them from the boxes even before they were divided up by O'Bryan to his fellow squad members. Theft of these luxury items was a capital offense. He shared a bunker with Renarie and many believed the big Italian would kill him before the North Vietnamese did.

"What is it, Borden?"

"We can't bathe at all, not even with a wet towel?"

"Not even with a wet towel, Borden."

"Any more questions? Okay, that's it. I'll be around to check on you guys later. I better not find anyone asleep on watch."

Nguyen once again was summoned back to the headquarters of the regimental commander, Col. Linh. Nguyen and his other two team members found the going extremely slow through the thick underbrush jungle. There was no other choice, however, since using the only road in the area would have invited attack from the air.

Nguyen stopped, squatted on the jungle floor, and began to check his bearings with his map and compass. He had traveled a large arch south and west of the American base at Lang Vei. He did not want any enemy patrols to stumble onto his tiny group. Col. Linh's headquarters had moved in his absence and now was located about 2000 meters southwest of the American base at Lang Vei.

He put away his map and compass, took a drink from his canteen, and then motioned to his team to resume their march. As he moved, he noticed that the jungle was quiet. There seemed to be no animals or even birds in the trees. He knew that men were somewhere nearby and hoped they were his comrades. For thirty minutes Nguyen and his two companions picked their way carefully through the dense underbrush. He stopped every few minutes to listen and smell the air. The Americans had peculiar odors, which traveled with them. Sometimes, it was their cigarettes or food they ate. Sometimes, it was just their distinctive body odors. There were no airborne alerts today.

Finally, the faint voices of North Vietnamese could be heard in the distance. Nguyen consulted his map again. The regiment should be located to his front (west) about 150 meters away on either side of a stream bed.

He and his men crawled forward to the crest of a small hill overlooking an even smaller plateau which the stream bed dissected. From this vantage point, Nguyen could see freshly dug holes and men sitting under a thick canopy of trees. Some of the men were cooking food, and some were asleep. Then Nguyen saw something that completely surprised him. Under the trees, hidden with a makeshift camouflage of tree limbs and brush, sat at least twenty tanks. *How did they get those here?* he thought.

Nguyen and his team stood up and walked down the bushy hillside into the camp. As he walked, he glanced at soldiers who seemed to pay his team little notice. He wondered, *Where are the sentries for this camp?*

It disturbed him that he and his men had walked

undetected into the middle of a regimental headquarters. *At least, there are no signs of tracks made by the tanks,* he thought with some consolation. *It will be nearly impossible for the American planes to spot them.*

"I need to report to Col. Linh," Nguyen told a young soldier who was cleaning his rifle. "Where is his command post?" The young soldier stood and pointed to a well concealed bunker under a stand of trees along the side of a stream.

As Nguyen approached the bunker, Col. Linh appeared from a ramped doorway, which was the bunker entrance. Nguyen approached the colonel. "Lt. Nguyen and scout team reporting as you ordered."

"Good to see you and your men, Lieutenant," the colonel replied. "Please get something to eat and then report back here to me. I have a mission for you and your men."

"Yes, sir," Nguyen replied.

In an hour, Nguyen returned to the colonel's bunker by himself. His men had washed in the stream and eaten some rice. Now they lay sound asleep under the shade of the thick trees next to the stream.

The colonel sat on a small camp stool with a map on his lap. Three other officers who were unknown to Nguyen stood around the colonel. The colonel was motioning with his hand toward the map, "The tanks will assault from two sides at once, accompanied by your infantry. We will also lay down a barrage of artillery and mortar fire as the assault begins."

Nguyen stopped walking and stood a respectful distance from the group of senior officers. What the group was discussing sounded like a large assault, and he hoped his mission would be part of whatever it was.

The group of officers took turns looking at the map over the colonel's shoulder. Nguyen heard the name, Lang Vei, mentioned several times. He recognized the name. It was the small American base he had taken the trouble to skirt on the way to this meeting. About five minutes later, the other officers began to take their leave of Col. Linh.

Linh turned to Nguyen, "Lt. Nguyen, come here and I will brief you on your mission." The colonel rose and placed the unfolded map on the camp stool then turned to face Nguyen.

"As you know, we have had to modify our plans some. We had planned to overrun the American outpost on hills 861 and 881 and then bring a full regiment to bear on the north side of Khe Sanh from these hills. Simultaneously, we would overrun the Khe Sanh village and the small camp here at Lang Vei," he said, pointing to the map.

Col. Linh took a deep breath, then continued, "Well, the assault on 881 was preempted. The Americans attacked us. They hit us while we were staging to attack them. The reinforced battalion of our men was severely reduced due to artillery and air strikes. Our force was compelled to withdraw with many dead and wounded. Two battalions did attack the hill 861 outpost that evening. Our sappers penetrated the American, and we overran half of their base. However, the Americans counter-attacked and killed or wounded many of our men. We were again forced to retreat. The Americans disrupted or destroyed much of our reinforcing battalion with artillery fire. Many of our men were trapped between the American artillery fire and their counter-attacking infantry."

He paused and exhaled deeply. "Our assault force was

wiped out." Nguyen's heart sank as the colonel pointed to the map with his index finger while describing the disastrous events.

The colonel continued, "This was all very disruptive to our plans. Our forces overran the Americans at Khe Sanh village but could go no further. We were to attack the Americans at Lang Vei, but the attack was not to start until the Americans on the hills had been destroyed. This has all caused us to make significant changes. We were to attack the Khe Sanh base from the north and the southwest with at least four regiments after an intense artillery and rocket barrage. Of course, this is not possible now."

Nguyen nodded his understanding.

"We have to alter our plans, and this, Lieutenant, is where your mission fits in," Linh said bending over the map. "Do you see this hill here just east of 861?"

"Yes," answered Nguyen.

"This is now occupied by the Americans. You will report to Col. Lang. Your mission is to take your scouts into the area, identify the key American positions, and report them to Lang's battalion commanders. You and your men will also be responsible for staking out the assembly areas for our troops to attack from. I have picked you because of your unique knowledge of the area."

"Yes, sir," Nguyen replied, studying the map intently.

"The information and maps you made of the Americans on 861 were very accurate. You do very good work, Nguyen."

"Thank you, sir," Nguyen replied, a little embarrassed at his commander's praise. "Sir," Nguyen said, hesitating, "what about the other two hills, 881 and 861? This hill," he pointed to the map, "will be of little use unless we control the other two hills."

Col. Linh smiled, "You are right, Nguyen. That is why I am assembling another regiment for these assaults. We will take all of these hills at the same time. My regiment will overrun the base at Lang Vei. The marines at Khe Sanh will send a rescue force, and we will be waiting for them on the road. We will annihilate them, then proceed to attack Khe Sanh from the southwest. Our men, after securing the hills, will be reinforced and sweep down on the base from the north in a coordinated attack. The marines at Khe Sanh will have a choice then to surrender or die. This will be the turning point of the war, Nguyen."

Nguyen studied the map in silence. It was a complex plan, and each phase depended on the success of the other. He knew from what Linh had told him that his superiors had underestimated the marines once already. The attacking forces sent against the hill outposts had not been large enough. He hoped this plan would not repeat the same mistake. "Very well, sir, when do I leave?"

"You and your men leave tomorrow. You will meet the troops organizing here," Ling said, pointing at a spot on the map north of hill 881. "You will then lead them into their staging areas for the attacks."

"Yes, sir," Nguyen replied.

"One more thing, Nguyen," Linh said as he gathered up the map. "You are not to take part in the actual assault, Lieutenant."

"Why not, sir?"

"I need you and your scouts for other missions. Your knowledge of the area and American positions is too valuable to me. You report back to me when this is finished."

"Yes, sir," Nguyen replied. He then turned to walk away.

"Lieutenant," called Linh.

"Yes, sir," he said, turning.

"Good luck."

Nguyen smiled back and walked away. *I am going to need lots of luck,* he thought.

O'Bryan and five of his squad members shoveled in the hard red clay. The hole was taking shape after three hours of digging the outline of a twelve-foot-wide by twelve-foot-long bunker that was now begging to emerge. O'Bryan was only able to find two real shovels. The others toiled with the small entrenching tools provided to each marine. The hole was now about three feet deep. The going was hard and slow, and O'Bryan's men cursed the ground, the North Vietnamese, and the Marine Corp. equally for their misfortune.

Renarie stood leaning against his shovel. "Time for a smoke break?" he asked.

O'Bryan paused, bent over with a shovelful of dirt. "Renarie, you spend more time on smoke breaks than you do digging. If you're tired, give the shovel to someone else and grab an entrenching tool."

"Take it easy, Corporal!" Renarie said while resuming his shoveling. "I was only askin'!"

Crack! A sniper round flew past just inches over Renarie's head. Instantly, they all flattened out in the hole. "Son of a bitch!" yelled Renarie face down in the dirt.

O'Bryan rose to his knees. "Anybody hit?" he asked,

looking around. "That's it for today. We'll wait till the fog comes back in the morning before we dig some more on this thing."

The roar of four giant engines sounded overhead. O'Bryan looked and saw a C-130 aircraft coming in on a steep angle approach to the Khe Sanh runway. The runway was the bullseye of the base. Rockets and mortar rounds began to impact along the plane's glide path.

CHAPTER FOURTEEN

"Shiiiiit!"

Jack Casey jumped from the rear ramp of the C-130 transport screaming as loud as he could and ran for his life. The explosions of 122mm rockets and 82mm mortar rounds raining down on him were muffled by the roar of the four-engine camouflaged, giant aircraft. Brown puffs marking the impacts on the corrugated runway sprang up around him as he struggled to escape the center of the Khe Sanh bullseye.

He sprinted, dragging his overstuffed issued green seabag by its strap, which contained all that he owned. The bag threw him off balance and caused him to fall, saving his life, as a rocket round slammed into the revving engine of the airplane behind him. A hot shock wave, smelling of airplane fuel, washed by and then chunks of metal whined over his head waist high.

Casey looked up to see bits of uniform along with black and red flesh, which had been the marine running behind him, spray past. He curled into a ball, pulled the big seabag close, and buried his face in the side of it. The noise of the combined explosions had reached a crescendo beyond hearing and left him in a numb ringing silence. Over this inferno, he heard a voice. At first, he thought it might be God.

"You hit?" Someone grabbed his right shoulder and rolled him over. Casey looked up to see an incredibly filthy corpsman crouching over him with a slick green waterproof medical kit.

"No, I don't think so."

"Then, you better get your ass off this runway, or you will be."

The corpsman reached down and pulled Casey to his feet, then turned and ran toward the burning hulk of the C-130.

Casey ran from the runway, still dragging his bag toward a trench line, which ran parallel to the runway about thirty meters away. He could hear more screaming rockets coming in and dove head first the last five meters into the trench line as the rockets exploded randomly on the airstrip behind him.

The trench was surprisingly deep, and it seemed to take a long time for him to hit the bottom. He lay there stunned for some time. After regaining his senses, he sat up and looked both directions down the trench line. He was alone in this section, which curved about forty feet to his right.

He inspected his arms and legs for damage and felt the top of his head. Other than scraped arms and a bump on his forehead from his swan dive into the trench, he was uninjured. He felt around next to him in the red dirt and found his glasses. Even with the elastic strap across the back, they had been knocked from his face and one lens was broken.

He felt wet and looked down to see red dirt caked to his crotch and along the inside of his leg. Somewhere between the time he left the plane and the time he arrived in the trench, he had wet himself. He could hear men shouting on the airstrip and positioned himself on a step, dug a few feet up into the trench wall, so that he could see over the top.

One of the oldest, most dilapidated fire trucks he had

ever seen had appeared on the runway and was spraying foam on the smoldering carcass of the four-engine aircraft. Marines and C. B.s with axes were on top of the fuselage chopping at the smoke-filled cockpit attempting to rescue a trapped pilot and co-pilot. Mortar rounds exploded on the runway as corpsmen and other marines scurried, bent over close to the ground, dragging the wounded away in ponchos.

These were, he thought, easily the bravest men he had ever seen in his life. He felt proud of them. He glanced to his right and noticed a makeshift sandbagged control tower which held a big red sign with yellow letters that read "WELCOME TO KHE SANH". He started to pull himself out of the trench to go and help but decided against it. *I don't even have a helmet or a flak jacket yet.*

Casey squinted down at his watch through his one unbroken lens. As near as he could figure, he had been on the ground at Khe Sanh now for twenty minutes. Less than seventy-two hours ago, he had been in Los Angeles eating a hamburger. He sat quietly and waited for his pants to dry.

A quarter mile away at the other end of the base, O'Bryan knelt down behind a four-foot sandbag wall, which surrounded an M60 machine gun emplacement. The incoming rocket and artillery fire had slacked off after a two-hour bombardment, but mortar and sniper fire still remained to harass the marines. It was time to go to the company C. P. (command post) and draw the daily cases of C-ration chow for his squad.

This meant leaving the relative safety of the eight-foot interconnecting trench lines and crossing a forty-foot open space. Snipers on the surrounding mountain sides had already shot two people in his platoon today. He surveyed the open ground and plotted a course that would not leave him in the open for more than a few seconds at a time. He hoped there wouldn't be an N.V.A. rocket or artillery barrage while he was in the open. Adrenaline began to surge and his legs tingled like a sprinter in the blocks, tensing in anticipation of the starter's gun.

"Hey, O'Bryan!" a voice with a thick Boston accent yelled. "You goin' to draw chow sometime today or not?"

"LCpl. Renarie, why don't you bring your fat ass out here and run over to the company C.P.?"

O'Bryan placed one hand on the sandbag wall and prepared to vault over.

"Didn't one of them replacements in the other squad get shot by a sniper this morning?"

O'Bryan paused and turned to look back at the trench line. He knew this voice, too. It belonged to a five foot, four inch slender blond with a choir boy face. It was Borden, the "little fuck."

"He sure did, Borden. You assholes that have been here for awhile are supposed to kind of take care of those guys until they figure out what's goin' on here."

"Hey, we told the guy. Didn't we, Borden?"

"Yeah, we told him," agreed Borden.

"Don't go stickin' your fuckin' head up."

"Guys in the other squad said when the plane got hit on the runway this morning, what's his name, the deceased new guy, had to stand up and see the big fireball. Sure as shit sniper shot him right through the fuckin' throat. Not our fault. We told him."

O'Bryan shook his head. "I know, Renarie. You told him."

"Anyway, before you go, since the new guy ain't gonna be eatin', guys in the squad thought maybe you could draw his chow still, and we could split it up."

O'Bryan smiled, "What a bunch of assholes."

He pushed himself over the gun pit wall and sprinted in a zigzag pattern bent low to the ground. He reached the safety of the next bunker wall then repeated his run to a mortar gun pit and then finally to the entrance of the company C.P. bunker.

The sniper fired, but he was too late. O'Bryan was already inside the company bunker. Lt. Henderson and Gunny Timmons looked up as he rushed in.

"Son of a bitch is slowin' up today...bet it's the same little bastard got our people this mornin'."

"Well, I'm a little harder to hit, Gunny. Ever try to shoot somethin' two inches off the ground doin' forty miles an hour?"

O'Bryan's eyes gradually adjusted to the dim light in the bunker. Lt. Henderson and Gunny Timmons sat on bunks made from artillery ammunition crates along opposite walls of the bunker. Henderson walked to the far end of the bunker where candles illuminated a makeshift table that supported radio equipment and a large clear plastic map board. He reached and picked up a sheet of paper from the table.

"Where's the captain?" asked O'Bryan.

"He's out checking the lines. Since you are the first squad leader here, I need you to go up to the battalion headquarters and pick up a replacement."

O'Bryan looked at the paper handed to him. It was a check-in sheet of places the new man needed to go. "Did he come in on the C-130 that got blown up this morning?"

"Same one," the Lieutenant replied. "There was another replacement for him, but he bought it when the plane got hit...never made it past the grave's registration bunker next to the strip. If this replacement seems OK, you can have him as your radio operator."

"Alright, sir, I'll go get him, but I hate goin' above ground this time of day...just about time for the evening appearance of the rockets. Where the hell has this guy been all day?"

"Somebody found him sittin' in a trench up behind the airstrip...said he got lost...had no gear. So, he just waited for someone to come along. I can understand that...hell of a place to drop into."

O'Bryan took the check-in sheet for the new man and turned to leave the bunker. The routine piece of paperwork seemed oddly out of place under the present circumstances. *I never thought of having to check into a battle,* he thought.

"Corporal."

"Yes, sir," O'Bryan stopped at the bunker entrance and turned to face the lieutenant.

"I hear that's the last plane that's gonna try to fly in here. From now on all our re-supply will be done by parachute. That means no more replacements for awhile. Try to keep this one alive longer than forty-eight hours."

"Yes, sir, but my men will be disappointed."

"Why's that?"

"No extra C-rats."

It took O'Bryan ten minutes to cover the quarter mile

to the battalion command post bunker, seeking shelter along the way from incoming rocket and sniper fire. He saw Casey sitting wild-eyed in a trench outside the battalion C.P. bunker, flanked by his green seabag and a red nylon mail bag.

"You the replacement for B Company?"

Casey stood slowly, "Yeah."

"Grab the mail and your bag. We got places to go and people to see. Stay close to me, and I'll try to keep you alive long enough to draw all your gear and ammunition."

Casey shadowed O'Bryan as they moved quickly from one trench line to the next. Huge metal shipping containers buried in the ground along a trench line served as Battalion Supply. Casey was issued a helmet, flak jacket, gas mask, pack, cartridge belt, canteens, rifle, and magazines. "I'll give you 300 rounds of ammunition when we get to our sector of the trench," O'Bryan said. He studied Casey as they prepared to leave the safety of the shipping container for the trip back above ground to the platoon positions on the south edge of the base perimeter.

He could barely see Casey inside the gear he was wearing and carrying. At most, Casey was five feet, seven inches tall and weighed no more than 130 pounds.

"Can you run inside there?"

Casey's helmet nodded up and down.

"Give me the mail bag." Casey handed it over. "Now, sling the rifle across your shoulders and lift the seabag on your back. We're gonna be movin' fast and low."

Casey followed O'Bryan over the debris strewn landscape. He tripped and stumbled over things he could only guess at as the deep mountain darkness spread over them. He was mesmerized by the shadowy figure of

O'Bryan in front of him. He seemed to glide over the rubble without effort. *A creature superbly adapted to this hell,* he thought. It was pitch black when they reached the platoon C.P. bunker. O'Bryan lifted a rubber poncho, which covered the bunker entrance, and pushed Casey inside into the candlelight.

Lt. Henderson and the platoon sergeant, Sgt. Tores, sat on wooden ammo crates eating from cans of C-rations. Henderson stood as they came down the incline from the bunker entrance to the dirt floor. O'Bryan dropped the red mail bag at the lieutenant's feet.

"Good work. You made it with the replacement and some mail. What's your name, Private?"

Casey dropped his sea bag and snapped to attention throwing up a quick salute. "Private Casey, sir."

"Where you from, Casey?"

"Upstate New York, sir."

"My name is Henderson, Lt. or Mr. will do, and we don't salute anyone in the field out here...just tells the enemy who to shoot first. This is Sgt. Tores. He is your platoon sergeant." Tores looked up momentarily at Casey with a mouth full of food and grunted a greeting.

Henderson continued, "How much education you have?"

"B.A....in philosophy."

"How long you been in the Corps?"

"Seven months."

"Draftee?"

"No, I volunteered."

Lt. Henderson shook his head. "Just what we need, a platoon philosopher. You're now O'Bryan's radio operator." Henderson turned to O'Bryan, "He's all yours,

O'Bryan. Show him his bunker. Pass the word out there: mail call in the morning. It will give them something to look forward to."

O'Bryan led Casey to the trench line down to his bunker. Along the way, Casey caught glimpses of his new home by the flickering light of huge magnesium flares dropped by DC-3 aircraft and flying in blackout overhead. The flares were suspended by swaying parachutes. He saw and heard other men, but they were only voices and movement in the shadows.

"You stay here in the bunker with me," O'Bryan motioned with his left arm. "This side is mine. Throw your stuff anywhere on that side." Casey threw his bag into the darkness on the right and heard it hit, knocking loose dirt from the damp bunker wall. O'Bryan fumbled in the dark then handed Casey a candle.

"Wait till I get the poncho pulled down over the doorway then light the candle. I got to go check on the squad."

When O'Bryan returned, he found Casey lying on his back on a rubber air mattress staring at the runway matting and sandbag ceiling. O'Bryan immediately blew out the candle.

"Don't leave the candle burning for no reason. Candles are worth their weight in gold. See you found the extra rubber lady."

"Rubber what?"

"Air mattress."

"Oh, yeah, and while I was blowing it up, I saw a huge gray rat...big as a cat!"

"I know," O'Bryan said while adjusting his rubber lady and poncho liner. "He lives here. I named him Pierre,

Powerful Pierre. I decided he might be one of those dead French soldiers reincarnated. All the B-52 raids and shelling drove the rats out of the countryside. They're not dumb, though. They came inside the perimeter and got down in the bunkers with us. See, Pierre just don't want to get killed by the gooks again. Just sleep with your boots and gloves on."

Casey crinkled his nose. "The smell around here is something else."

"Really?" O'Bryan sniffed. "I wondered if it smells here. None of us have bathed, shaved, or changed clothes in a long time. It's because of the water shortage. Water is for drinking only. If I catch you bathin' or shavin' with it, you're in deep shit."

"I'm not talking about that smell. I know that smell, but it's something else. It's something between rot and mildew."

"Well, there's a lot of dead and dying people around here. Probably has somethin' to do with it."

Casey was silent for a moment. "You think I can really get used to this?"

"You'll be amazed at what you can get used to, Casey. Get some sleep. I didn't put you on watch tonight. First night's on the house."

Casey was silent but wide awake. Occasionally, a marine 105 or 155 howitzer fired from their positions thirty to forty yards away, and dirt would fall from the sandbags on to Casey's face. He placed his helmet over his face to try and counter the falling dirt. He could hear the rat moving between the sandbags overhead.

"O'Bryan?"

"What?"

"I can hear the rat. I don't have any gloves."

"It could be a lot worse, Casey. You could be up on one of those hills. The N.V.A. has been hittin' them with massed attacks. They nearly overran Hill 861. The fightin' was hand-to-hand up there."

"Do you think that will happen here, Corporal?"

"For sure, if those marines on the hills don't hold...maybe even if they do. Who knows."

"Shit!" Casey mumbled into his helmet.

"Put your hands in your pockets. Don't fuck with Pierre though. If he wakes you up in the middle of the night, give him whatever he wants." O'Bryan smiled, rolled over, and went instantly to sleep.

Moving quietly and quickly from dusk to dawn, Lt. Nguyen and his two scouts carefully made their way down the triple canopy covered mountainside. For several days, they had traversed the difficult terrain and were about to arrive at a point 2000 north of the marines on Hill 881 south.

They had traveled through nights so black they were forced to hold on to each other's cartridge belts in a single file in order to stay together. Sometimes, sporadic American artillery fire or aerial bombs would puncture the black void in random blasts, but nothing landed close to their little group.

Now exhausted and nearly out of water, they were looking down at two valleys on either side of a hill where a North Vietnamese regiment was encamped. The dense jungle undergrowth provided excellent coverage. From the air or the ground, the men were nearly invisible.

After making contact with an outpost, Nguyen reported to the regimental headquarter's bunker. He was ushered in to see a Col. Lang.

"Lieutenant, glad to see you arrived safely."

"Thank you, sir."

"You and your two men will act as guides for my battalion commanders. I want you to lead one group, a reinforced battalion, while your men will each lead a battalion."

Nguyen pulled out his plastic-encased map in the dim bunker light. "What is my objective, sir?"

The colonel paused for a moment searching the map. "Here," he said, pointing to a spot on Nguyen's map.

"That is very close to the American position on Hill 861."

"Yes, the enemy just recently occupied this. As you can see, it sits between 861 and this other enemy position on Hill 558. It appears to be small, no more than thirty to forty men. It shouldn't be difficult to deal with. We will hit at night, come out of the valley fog."

The colonel walked away from Nguyen and sat down in a small canvas folding chair, then continued, "Once your objective is overrun the men will sweep through and join the other battalion in the assault on 861. That will be a combined force of around 1500 men against maybe 200 Americans, a very good assault ratio. After the Americans on Hill 861 are reduced, the entire force joins the remaining battalion assaulting the Americans on 881. We will reduce these hills one at a time, bringing maximum force against each objective."

Nguyen smelled the rich decaying odor of the freshly

dug hole as he studied the map. He knew the area well and could picture the approach routes to the hills in his mind.

The colonel rose quickly from his chair. "Any questions about your assignment, Lieutenant?"

"No, sir," Nguyen replied. "I assume you will want me to lead our troops in from the northwest of this hill to negate the effect of artillery support from Khe Sahn?"

"Of course, Lieutenant, and I want you to do a reconnaissance to spot their crew-served weapons for our mortar teams."

"When do we start?"

"Tonight. Your group has further to travel. The other two battalions will leave tomorrow night."

"Yes, sir," Nguyen snapped and then turned to leave the headquarters and brief his men.

Nguyen led the column of just over 800 men of the Ninety-Fifth regiment down through the jungle valley floor. No one spoke in the pitch black night. Small pieces of white fluorescent tape were attached to the back of each man's pack. The men simply had to follow the man in front of him, except Nguyen. No one was in front of him.

He paused in a small stream bed on the valley floor. Overhanging vines and branches gave him the feeling of being in a large wet tunnel. The dense jungle held the heat from the day. As the night air cooled the ground, a misty fog began to form around them.

He struggled to see the luminous dials of his compass in order to get his heading straight. He thought about his travels in the past through this area. *A map is nearly useless at night in the jungle.* His own words while training scouts played back to him. *What we do is more of an art than science. The map you must depend on is in your head.* Something moved in the mist directly in front of him. There was almost no noise, but the swirling fog gave away movement. Whatever it was, it was huge. He sat quietly as the sound of a breaking vine and the movement of the swirling fog shifted away from him. *Tiger,* he thought. The hair on his neck raised.

He got his compass azimuth and continued along the shallow streambed. Behind him, a company of sappers and two battalions of infantry followed in a column nearly half a mile long. Looking down, he saw huge paw prints. He smiled. *I wonder if we are the hunters or the hunted.*

The sun began to rise and shone like a huge lighthouse fixed in fog. Nguyen halted. *We should be just behind a hill to their right about a mile from our objective.* He crawled forward to the top of a small rise to wait while the sun burned away the fog. *I wonder what she is doing now.* He felt an aching inside. A mental image of her smiling face floated in the white mist before him. "Thi," he mouthed, nearly saying her name out loud.

The shroud of fog gradually disappeared. He squatted and looked back over his shoulder. Though he could not see them, he knew that 800 men lay behind him, hidden in the low fog and thick underbrush. They would lie there all day, camouflaged by natural vegetation while their officers made last-minute plans for the coming night assault.

Nguyen crawled forward and surveyed the new Marine position with his field glasses. *The north is definitely the only approach for the assault. Good, the men are already in good positions for the attack.* The marines appeared to occupy a narrow salient directly to his front. He worried because he could not see how deep the Marine position went. However, he could clearly see a mortar position and several machine gun emplacements.

Just before dark, he directed an 82mm mortar to fire one round into the middle of the Marine positions. He observed the resulting explosion. When the assault began, he would make an adjustment in the mortar fire from where this single round landed. The marines seemed to ignore the mortar round. There was no return fire. Nguyen and the force he led lay motionless. Some tried to sleep, but few succeeded. Nguyen wondered if he would even see the sun again as darkness spread over him.

He raised his sleeve and looked at the luminous dials of his watch. It was 0258 hours. The attack was to commence at 0400 hours so that it would be coordinated with the attacks on the other two hills. He lay flat on his back swatting at insects buzzing around his face. Finally, he rose and looked toward the Marine position. The six-foot-high elephant grass blocked his view, so he walked to the top of a small hill facing the enemy line. He crouched on the hilltop looking for telltale light from the Marine bunkers.

The sky to the west of him suddenly exploded with silent white flashes. The fog made them appear like hazy lights in the distance. Then the thunder of hundreds of exploding artillery shells rolled echoing across the hills. Nguyen's stomach fluttered.

"Radio," he said reaching his hand towards a nearby radio operator who handed him the handset.

"Viper One to Viper Two or Three, come in!" Nguyen knew he was not to break radio silence, but the success of the whole operation might be hanging in the balance.

After a few minutes, he could make out a weak, "Viper

Two to Viper One." In the background were loud explosions mixed with the screams of men.

Nguyen quickly called again, "Viper One to Viper Two or Three, come in." There was no response. The sounds of the shelling in the distance grew more intense and sustained. The man-made thunderstorm built to a frenzy and continued for another twenty minutes. It was Nguyen's worst fear come true. *His scouts and the troops following them must have been caught in the open by the American artillery,* he thought.

He crawled forward to the assault staging positions of a 200-man sapper unit. The sapper's job was to breach the marines' wire and knock out any bunkers or crew-served weapons they could find. He noticed most of these men carried no rifles or packs. They carried only explosive charges and hand grenades. They were to come through the enemy wire during their own heavy mortar barrage, which Nguyen knew sadly he must direct.

He moved through the men and noticed them using syringes to inject each other with pain killers. It was crucial that they keep going even though they would all probably be wounded. Nguyen had much respect for these men. "Most of them," he thought, "will soon be dead."

He at last found a young captain in charge, checking the explosive charges his men would be carrying. "Captain, I think you should consider postponing the assault."

"Why?" the captain asked, frowning.

"The other battalions with which we are to coordinate our attack have been hit. Don't you hear that massive bombardment over the hill?"

The captain paused for a moment, listening. "Yes, but

it doesn't directly concern our mission. None of those men were to help us. After we wipe out these Americans, then we will help our brothers with the other two hills."

Nguyen shook his head in disbelief. He wondered if the young captain was already under the influence of the pain killer. "Good luck, Captain," he said and walked back to his small hilltop facing the soon-to-be battleground.

At 0400 hours, Lt. Nguyen raised his right hand and fired a red flare into the air. A huge volley from twelve 82mm mortars sounded from the valley behind him...then silence again in the black, moist night. From his small hill, Nguyen strained to see into the thick fog of the valley below him. From his small hill, Nguyen strained to see into the thick of the valley below him. The mortar rounds sailed in a high arch and impacted in a ragged series of red flashes accompanied by deep crump noises in the Marine hillside positions.

Nguyen rose to a bent standing posture trying to observe where the rounds landed, in order to direct the next barrage. Below the sapper, suicide assault had begun. He could hear men screaming and yelling. Explosions illuminated the Marine wire like small lightning strikes. "Drop fifty meters! Fire for effect!" he yelled into his radio handset.

Red tracers began to pour from the Marine machine gun positions on the long exposed finger of the hill. Nguyen watched with satisfaction as the explosions of the mortar rounds saturated the Marine positions. One by one, the red streams of tracers were extinguished as the machine guns were silenced. Illumination flares began to pop in the sky, casting eerie light and shadows across the hill.

Nguyen watched as the second wave of 200 men of the Ninety-Fifth infantry regiment surged through the wire breaches behind the advancing sappers. He saw the line of green tracer bullets, which his men used, begin to sweep up the hillside.

He grabbed the radio handset again. "Add seventy-five meters! Fire for effect...all guns!"

More illumination rounds popped over the hillside facing him as forty-eight more mortar rounds cashed farther up the hillside following his correction. Some men threw grenades, some fired rifles point-blank at each other. Then the night was black again and filled with screams and gunfire. The acrid smell of high explosives mixed with a faint burning sensation wafted across the small valley to him. *Tear gas,* he thought. *They are using tear gas.*

So far, everything is going well, Nguyen thought. The Marine's wire had been penetrated, and their crew-served weapons knocked out. The vanguard of the surviving sappers, backed by infantry, were advancing up the hills toward a large tree where he was nearly certain the enemy command post would be located. He looked over his shoulder to see if the 400 men of the second and third waves of the attack had begun to move out of their valley staging positions. Stray bullets cracked by his head, and he squatted quickly to the ground. He then popped back up erect to again catch a glimpse of the flare-illuminated battlefield chaos. From near the top of the hill, he saw a steady line of muzzle flashes, which raked the North Vietnamese trying to scale the hill. The increasing volume of fire made it clear to him that the marines were counter-attacking. The assault was faltering.

Nguyen scrambled to the radio. "Add fifty meters! Fire for effect! Fire until you are out of ammunition!" The last syllable he uttered was lost in a huge blinding red flash and roar. The last thing he remembered was the sensation of wind and flying through the air.

He awakened on the ground in a dense cloud of gray smoke with his ears ringing loudly. The sound of more explosions detonating around him shook the earth he lay on. Above the din, he could faintly hear jet engines roaring away.

In the quiet that followed, he could hear men moaning in the inferno which was now the valley below him. "Oh, God, help me! Mother, oh please, help me!" The chorus of groans and pleas for help continued but went unanswered in the night.

There will be no second or third wave, he thought.

Nguyen rose unsteadily to his knees and then staggered sideways back towards his previous position atop the small hill. Blood ran thickly down his left arm. He also wiped blood from his eyes and tasted its iron metallic stickiness on his tongue. Looking across, he could see the remnants of the assault force running back down the hill. The smell of cordite and burning flesh came up on a thin breeze from the valley behind him.

In front of him, a ghostly figure began to appear from the valley fog below. *Where's my rifle?* he thought. *Must find my rifle.*

"Lieutenant?" the figure called.

Flares popped across the valley. In the swaying light, Nguyen recognized the blood-smeared face of the young Sapper Captain.

"Lieutenant, where are the other assault waves? We

need more supporting fire!"

He could barely hear the captain over the incessant ringing in his ears. "In the valley behind me," he pointed, "but I think most of them are dead from aircraft bombs and artillery fire."

The captain walked past Nguyen as if he did not see him. "That can't be," the captain said as he disappeared over the hilltop to the carnage below.

Nguyen sat down heavily and tried to regain his senses. An aching, burning pain seemed to be centered just below his left shoulder. He removed his shirt and found a jagged slash, which half circled his upper arm. The bleeding from the small scalp wounds seemed to have slowed. He removed a field bandage from a pouch on his cartridge belt. Using his teeth to hold one end of the bandage, he tied the pressure wrap around his bleeding arm. Feeling light-headed, he lay on the ground. He slipped in and out of consciousness and had no idea how long he lay there.

The next thing he knew, the captain dropped to the ground next to him. "There's not much left of them," he said, squatting next to Nguyen. "Are you wounded badly, Lieutenant?" Nguyen sat upright, looking at the dark outline of the captain.

"It's not all that bad...just a deep cut. The shrapnel passed through my arm." Nguyen reached across with his right hand and covered the bandaged upper arm. He looked at the captain.

"Are they all dead?"

"Those who aren't, soon will be. It looks like they were forming into columns when the bombs hit. I saw a few blood trails in the elephant grass made by the wounded crawling away."

"What happened to your attack?" Nguyen asked.

"We overran half the hill, but the enemy position was bigger than we were told. They counterattacked from near the top of the hill and pushed us back down it into the valley. Over half my men are dead, and everyone is wounded. If the second and third wave had joined us, as we had planned, we would have annihilated them. Still, we killed many of them."

The swooshing sound of incoming artillery sent them both flat on the ground. Huge explosions and giant orange-white flashes lit the valley behind them.

"They have us trapped!" Nguyen yelled to the captain whose face was only six inches from his own.

The captain raised his head a few inches off the ground, "Where is that artillery fire coming from...not Khe Sanh?

"No!" Nguyen yelled back. "Not Khe Sanh...another base somewhere...big guns."

"They have us boxed in."

The captain rolled to his knees. "I am going to lead what's left of my new men against the enemy positions again. We have no choice. If we are still here when the sun comes up, we are completely exposed. You stay here, Lieutenant. Your orders were to guide us. I'll send for you when the hill is ours."

Nguyen watched as the Captain bolted up but bent low with his rifle and ran back to his men on the foggy valley floor. Nguyen curled into a ball on the hillside in the thick elephant grass. Artillery continued to pound the reverse slope of the hill and valley beyond with what he thought was an unending merciless chain of explosions. Echoing in his mind was the thought, *All dead...400 men.*

He looked at the luminous dials on his watch, 0600. Soon it would be light. Then he heard the attack begin again up the hillside.

Once again, the flares popped overhead. He stood and watched the captain leading his men up the hill. Heavy fire cut them down to a man within minutes. This time, they never breached the enemy wire. *Unbelievably brave but doomed,* he thought.

Nguyen sat and waited in quiet disbelief. No one came back. *No one is ever coming back,* he thought. Nearly a whole regiment was gone. He was alone.

The fog began to spread up the hillsides from the valley floor. He crawled down from his vantage point. Next to a dead body, he found a slightly damaged but usable AK-47 rifle. He began a long, slow journey west towards Hill 881. *I must tell the command what happened here,* he thought.

His arm had stopped bleeding but throbbed with excruciating pain beneath the pressure bandage. Each time a jungle vine caught him, he cursed to himself. He cursed the Americans, the war, and the stupidity of his own commanders. Artillery still crashed into the valley where the men had been staged for the attack. *Leave them alone. They're dead,* he thought. Tears made small furrows down his blood-crusted cheeks as he disappeared beneath the thick brush undergrowth.

CHAPTER FIFTEEN

Jack Casey awakened from a sound sleep to find himself pulled upright to a sitting position. For just a moment, he thought the huge rat, Pierre, had him. Then, O'Bryan's voice screamed out of the darkness inches from his face.

"Incoming, grab your rifle, flak jacket, helmet, and gas mask." Instantly, O'Bryan was gone into the trench.

Casey fumbled in the dark for his gear. He could not hear any explosions, only distant hollow metallic thumps over and over again. He found everything but his rifle and glasses in the dark when the rockets began to scream in and explode.

The explosions came over one after another in a rapid succession and blended together. Casey fell into the trench and began to crawl along the bottom on his hands and knees. The trench shook and dirt cascaded down the sides. He crawled blindly until he ran into O'Bryan and the other squad members huddled below a machine gun position in the trench.

"Pretty hot up there!" O'Bryan yelled pointing upward. "Lieutenant says to stay down. Wait and see if this is the big ground assault."

They laid in the trench for hours as wave after wave of rocket and artillery fire slammed in all around them. In the darkness, men's curses and screams melded with the screams of the Chinese and Russian rockets. Soon, Casey learned to tell how close the explosion would be by how long he heard the rocket scream down on them. One-tenth of an extra second meant an explosion within killing distance to them. Every so often, after a close one, he could hear the frantic call, "Corpsman! Corpsman!" Casey could not imagine himself running through the blasts above ground, but he knew the corpsman did. Time quickly lost all meaning to him. The rockets fell forever.

Then suddenly they stopped. All of them were deaf from the concussions and shouted at each other from a few feet away as they shook loose dirt from their clothing.

"Think it's over?" Casey shouted at O'Bryan.

"How the fuck should I know. I look like an N.V.A. general?"

"Cpl O'Bryan!" rang out from overhead in a voice that even those with ruptured ear drums could hear.

"Here, Gunny!" shouted O'Bryan.

"Have your people count off and then get back to their positions. One hundred percent watch the rest of the night. Have them ready to saddle-up if need be."

"Right, Gunny. What's the word?"

"Word is the N.V.A. are overrunnin' the Special Forces at Lang Vei. They got tanks, they may be comin' through with them right up the road to us."

"Second squad count off!" yelled O'Bryan.

Each man then yelled his number in the squad all down the trench up to Casey who shouted, "Fourteen."

O'Bryan turned to Gunny Tores, "All present and accounted for."

Tores sounded as relieved as O'Bryan had ever heard him. "Fucking amazing, all your people are in one piece. Be ready. This may be the night."

Casey followed O'Bryan to a sandbagged fighting position along the trench line. Steps had been cut into the side of the six-foot trench so that two men could stand on the steps and fire through openings in the sandbags along the top.

"Where is your rifle, Casey?"

"I guess it's in the bunker. Don't get upset. I'll find it in a minute. First, I have to find my glasses."

O'Bryan shook his head in disbelief. "Casey, how the hell did you end up here?"

"It's kind of complicated."

"You're definitely not cut out for this. I mean you got glasses thick as coke bottles. What exactly was it you were doing before you joined the Marines?"

Casey squinted at O'Bryan, trying to focus the blurry image of his face. "I was studying to be a Catholic monk at St. Augustine's in upstate New York."

"A what?"

"A monk, you know...like a priest."

"I know what a monk is."

"Well, I was just finishing my last year and was about to take my final vows: poverty, chastity, obedience, and all that."

"So, what happened? How did you end up here?"

"It's kind of embarrassing, but it doesn't seem to make much difference now. There were five of us about ready to take our final vows. We got permission to go into town and have dinner together. We found a nice little place and had steaks. I guess I had a little too much wine and got drunk. I wouldn't go back with the rest of them to the monastery. They left me, and I proceeded to get really drunk. What happened next is a little fuzzy. The next clear thing I remember is waking up back in my cell at the monastery. Brother Theodore, one of the teachers, is shaking me. I sit up, and there's a nude woman with blonde hair asleep next to me."

"No shit, Casey?"

"No shit."

"They kick you out?"

"That day."

"Ever see the girl again?"

"No, she got her clothes and walked away. Don't even know her name. My family has had a priest or a nun in every generation since the turn of the century until me. I couldn't go home and face my mother. I went back to town and got drunk again. When the Marine recruiting office opened in the morning, I was sitting on the steps. So, here I am."

"Go find your rifle and glasses, Casey."

O'Bryan stood on the dug out step and looked into the night. The artillery behind them was firing furiously in support of the beleaguered Special Forces camp. He thought about the story Casey had told him and began laughing out loud. It was the strangest story he had heard from one of his men so far.

Casey returned down from the trench line with his rifle in one hand and his glasses in the other hand. One lens of his glasses was missing, and they appeared deformed.

"Stepped on my glasses," Casey stated matter-of-factly. I think I can fix them, though, with some of that black electrical tape we got."

"You know, Casey, I been thinkin' about what you told me. Sounds to me like you came here to hide...maybe even get killed?"

"How long have you been over here, Corporal?"

"About fourteen months."

Casey sat down on the step next to where O'Bryan stood. He began trying to get the bent glasses straight across his nose. "So then, you extended your tour six months. You've been over here, and you don't have to be either."

"Yeah, but that's different. This is what I do for a living. I'm a Marine. Besides, I've lost some friends over here. I don't think things are even yet between me and the N.V.A. out there!"

"Do you know what a Catholic priest does, O'Bryan?"

"Sure. I went to church once."

"He makes sacrifices on an altar."

Casey paused, took his right index finger, and shoved his broken glasses back in place on his nose. "Look around you. Not all the altars are inside churches."

O'Bryan glanced down at Casey. "My job is to try to keep my men alive, which means to kill as many of the other bastards as I can. Go fix your glasses. When it gets light, we may be going to Lang Vei."

Thick fog was beginning to show in the soft dawn light. Casey scooted off the step and into the trench, quickly disappearing in the fog.

By 10:00 a.m., the fog had burned off. Stragglers from the overrun Special Forces camp at Lang Vei began to arrive at the base. The word was passed by the lieutenant that they would not be going to Lang Vei. The Army said the North Vietnamese had withdrawn, leaving behind seven dead tanks. Ragged looking refugees began to arrive at Khe Sanh along with the sixteen Special Forces survivors. The refugees were halted outside the northwest entrance to the base because there were said to be infiltrators among them. O'Bryan took Casey and went to the ammunition re-supply point where he drew eight L.A.A.W. rockets for his squad. Casey helped him carry them back on the rubble-strewn dirt road that ran somewhat parallel to the airstrip.

"Ever fire one of these things, Casey?"

"Sure, once in infantry training."

O'Bryan pulled one of the disposable anti-tank rockets from his shoulder. "Quick refresher, Casey," he said, holding out the rocket. "Pull this pin and the tube telescopes out. Pull this next pin and the sight pops up. This last pin is the safety. Pull it and it's armed. Squeeze down on this plastic trigger on top and it fires. Got it?"

"Sure," said Casey, "three pins then fire."

O'Bryan slung the rocket by its carrying strap back over his shoulder. "Good, you're now an antitank man. Just don't pull on anything until I give you the word." O'Bryan had a brief mental image of Casey blowing up the whole squad practicing with his L.A.W.

They both paused and looked up as an F-4 Phantom jet made a low pass over the base. Two more Phantoms made bombing runs. The napalm blossomed like hideous black and orange flowers on the hillside.

"That ought to keep the snipers down," Casey remarked.

"Yeah, it's a good day," O'Bryan replied. "I think we got some mail today, too."

After passing out the L.A.A.W. rockets to his squad in the trench line, O'Bryan held mail call. He gave Casey a copy of *Time* magazine provided by the U.S.O. Then he sat down next to him on the edge of the trench. He held a letter in his hand addressed to John O'Bryan with no return address. His pulse quickened as he looked at the handwriting. It was a letter from her. He knew her handwriting. Susan Williams had said she never wanted to see him again. Was this written confirmation of what she said to him at the airport? All of these things ran through his head at once. He slipped down into the trench and walked a little away from Casey and the other men for privacy. He then ripped open the light blue envelope with the delicate scrawls:

Dear John,

I am furious with you. You must be the most stubborn, pig-headed person I have ever personally met. Do not write me, call me, or in any way contact me until you come back from Vietnam.

Having said all that...I love you, miss you, and worry about you constantly. Damn you! How dare you do this to me! Please come home.

Love,
Susan

P.S. Call me from the airport in L.A. when you are home. I will pick you up.

"Good news?" asked Casey.

O'Bryan quickly folded the letter and stuck it in the deep side pocket of his jungle utility pants. "I have never seen a smile that big on your face."

"Just a letter from a friend," replied O'Bryan.

"Must be some friend." Casey held out the *Time*

magazine to O'Bryan. "Finished this. Never thought I would get occupant mail over here. The news is not good. *Time* says we are in imminent danger of being overrun and wiped out, just like the French at Dien Bien Phu." O'Bryan took the magazine and began to thumb through it.

"Fuck the French!" yelled Renarie from the machine gun emplacement. Another voice down the trench line yelled, "Fuck *Time* magazine!"

Someone else added, "Jane Fonda, too!"

Casey turned to O'Bryan, "Kind of strange reading about our impending demise in *Time* while we sit here waiting for them to come."

O'Bryan stood up. "Kind of like reading your own obituary?"

"Yeah," replied Casey. "You know, it really gives me the creeps...like seeing it in print makes it more likely."

O'Bryan paused for a moment and then looked up from the *Time* magazine. "Casey, do you really think you could kill someone when it comes down to it? I mean, you being a Catholic monk and everything."

Casey considered this for a moment, staring at O'Bryan. He pushed his glasses up straight on his nose. "I told you I wasn't a very good monk."

Nguyen made his way cautiously along a narrow path, which led to a rubber plantation slightly west and north of Khe Sanh village, some distance from the Khe Sanh base. The village had been abandoned by the Americans during the first week of the attack.

A company was sent to occupy the former South Vietnamese District Headquarters. Col. Linh had told him that this would be a rally point in the event that he or his men became separated.

During the night, from a high hillside, he had witnessed an awesome sight, an American B-52 bombing raid two miles west of him. The bombs had fallen without warning in a cascade of fury on the Army Headquarters in the Co Roc area. Even from a distance, it was frightening. He had traversed across hills where B-52s had struck. The land looked as if a giant beast had walked across it leaving cratered footprints and even changed the course of rivers. He doubted anyone underneath that hell could have survived.

As he moved along the path in twilight, he began to smell the sickening, pungent odor of burning flesh. Rounding a bend in the path, he spotted neat, well-spaced rows of rubber trees. Something was wrong. If this was a rally point and patrol base for a hundred North Vietnamese soldiers, there should be sentries on checkpoints.

He looked at the trees more closely. They were burnt, and the earth around them was scorched. As he drew closer, the smell was overwhelming. Then he saw the scarred face of a man and a leg protruding from the side of a tree.

His eyes grew wide, and his hand went instinctively to cover his mouth and nose. Burnt rubber trees and bodies of soldiers were fused together in a grotesque fashion everywhere he looked. It all became clear to him. The soldiers had sought cover and camouflage by huddling under the trees as American jets approached. The jets must have dropped some of the giant 1000-pound napalm canisters. The result had been an enormous napalm fireball, which killed them all in an instant. The flash fire had frozen each man in his death throes. Some of the figures were kneeling, some were standing and some were prone on the ground. In the fading light, the result was a macabre forest of melded trees and men. Nguyen wretched and then began to run. He ran until his lungs ached, and he was clear of the burnt plantation. Then, exhausted, he stopped along a dirt road which led to the American base at Lang Vei. He crawled into some high weeds next to the road and lay down. The agonized screaming faces in the rubber trees haunted him throughout the night.

In the dawn light, Nguyen thought he heard someone coming down the dirt road. The morning fog was still thick, and he thought, *I am safe here as long as I don't move.* The footsteps on the road, a mere ten feet away, grew closer. He wished that he had stopped to pry a rifle from one of the hundreds of dead he had seen the last two days. All he could do now was lie motionless holding his breath. He exhaled, and a wave of relief washed over him as he heard the singsong dialect of two North Vietnamese soldiers draw even with him on the road. "Don't shoot! Don't shoot!" he shouted, stumbling to his feet. "I am Lt. Nguyen, Scout Sniper's Unit."

The eight-man patrol flattened on the dirt road with every rifle trained on him as he emerged from the tall grass. The patrol leader, a sergeant, slowly rose to his feet and approached Nguyen. "Where is your weapon, Lieutenant?"

"I lost it during a bombing two days ago. All the troops

I was with are dead. It is important that I find Col. Linh."

"Do you have any water?"

"I have had no water for over a day."

The sergeant unslung a canteen carried by a strap over his shoulder and handed it to Nguyen.

"I don't think you will be able to speak with Col. Linh. He died two days ago during the attack on Lang Vei."

Nguyen lowered the canteen from his lips.

"The colonel is dead?"

"Yes, killed by machine gunfire as he lead us in the attack."

"Was the attack successful?"

"Yes," the sergeant added affirmatively. "We defeated the Americans and their paid mercenaries. But the cost was high. Even with the tanks, it was a hard fight. We waited in an ambush for the marines to come and help them, but they never came. There was no attack on Khe Sanh. We lost seven of our tanks, and half our men were killed or wounded. There just weren't enough of us left to attack Khe Sanh."

Nguyen looked at the small ragged group of men standing around him. They did not look like victors. "I was with the Ninety-Fifth Regiment. We were to attack and overrun the Marine hill positions. The battalion I was with was destroyed. Nearly all of them are dead."

The sergeant took the canteen back from Nguyen. "Come with us. We are in a new position, which we dug just west of the American base at Khe Sanh. We are dug in waiting for replacement and resupply. I will take you to our captain and you can give him your report."

Nguyen fell in behind the eight men who turned and walked single file into the thick undergrowth. He hoped that they were not going very far. His legs were shaky, and he felt light-headed from hunger.

He noticed immediately that they were headed back along the same way he had just come. "Sergeant, where are you going now?"

The sergeant paused and looked back at him. "Before we return, we are going to check on a company from our battalion. After we drove the Americans from Lang Vei, they were sent to the Frenchman's rubber plantation to secure our flank from attack from the north."

Nguyen looked at the ground for a moment. "There is no need to go there. I just came through the rubber plantation. They are all dead, hit by napalm bombs."

"All? Surely someone survived!"

"Take my word, Sergeant," Nguyen said, grabbing the sergeant's arm. "They are all dead. There is no one there to contact."

The little column turned around and headed back to the narrow dirt road. No one spoke. Nguyen thought, *We are all probably dead, too. We just don't know it yet.*

Chapter Sixteen

The weather cleared in the afternoon. Forward air control teams called in swarms of F-4 Phantoms to pound the hills and valleys around Khe Sanh. O'Bryan used this opportunity to get the men back to work on the super bunker. Half the squad filled sandbags with the red dirt from the now twelve-foot-deep hole. Casey O'Bryan, Borden, and Renarie dug at the bottom of the hole.

Casey paused and looked around at the 12 x 12 x 12 hole. "You know, there is something biblical about this," he said with a flourish of his right hand.

Renarie looked up at this remark. "You mean like the slaves buildin' the fuckin' pyramids?"

"No, no, I mean like Noah and the flood. This is our ark. We shall survive catastrophe in it!"

"Bullshit," Renarie spat. "There was no one shootin' at Noah with any 122mm rockets."

"OK, OK," O'Bryan interrupted. "It's time to go bring the runway matting over.

Everyone dropped their shovels and headed to the trench line where the stolen sections of corrugated steel runway matting were stored. O'Bryan and Gage carried the first piece down the steep ramp into the hole.

"Okay, now you see what we're doin', Casey? This hole at the bottom of the hole is our protection from cave-ins. If the shit starts landin' close, we jump in this hole inside the bunkers and pull the runway matting over us."

Casey looked at the four by six-foot hole on the bunker floor. "I get it," he said. "A bunker inside a bunker."

"That's it," beamed O'Bryan.

"I'm just worried about one thing, O'Bryan."

"What's that?"

"How much air you figure we got in that hole? If this bunker caves in on us, it might be awhile before anyone digs us out."

"Don't worry about it, Casey. If that happens, the blast will probably kill us anyway. But there's always the chance we might survive down there."

After another four hours work, the runway matting roof and two layers of sandbags were in place over the top of the huge hole. The men stood around the bunker admiring their work.

"OK, that's it for today," O'Bryan announced. "Tomorrow, we put four more layers of sandbags on the roof and another layer of runway matting. Then, we move in."

"I can't wait," said Borden. "Maybe, we will have it all to ourselves for awhile. I'd like to move in before the rats do."

"Me too," Casey agreed.

The thump of mortar tubes in the distance sent everyone running for the safety of the trench line. Moments later, 82mm motar rounds began impacting one after another in the slow progression across the compound. No sooner had these rounds exploded than the hollow thump of rockets and artillery sounded in the distance. The rockets screamed down mixed with what had to be at least ten 130mm artillery rounds. It began like all the other barrages they had endured, but this time, it was different.

"Shit! They hit the ammo dump again!" yelled O'Bryan. Unexploded artillery shells flew overhead making strange wobbly whistling sounds. Wave after wave of artillery and rockets saturated the base as darkness began to fall. O'Bryan, Casey, and the rest of the squad lay huddled in the trench. Beehive rounds for 106mm recoilless rifles cooked off in the dump showering the area with thousands of small metal darts.

"Motherfucker!" yelled Renarie. "Get this shit off me!" he screamed, as he held up his right arm. O'Bryan quickly reached and began to pick out the tiny darts stuck in Renarie's arm.

"I been wounded, Corporal. Look at all these wounds. I need to be medevacked outta of here."

"Shut up, Renarie. You ain't goin' anywhere with these little pissy holes. Look. These darts are barely stuck in your arm."

"Well, at least it's a Purple Heart."

"Purple Heart my ass, Renarie. I seen you cut yourself worse shavin'. Purple Hearts are for guys who are really wounded."

The debate was cut short by more rockets exploding next to the trench and showering everyone with dirt and dust.

Hour after hour, the pounding continued.

"I think we may be goin' for the record!" yelled O'Bryan over the noise of nearby explosions.

"What record?" yelled Casey who sat on the bottom of the trench next to O'Bryan.

"The record for most incoming rounds in Vietnam. Believe it or not, there are guys sittin' around here right now whose job is to count how many rounds are bein' fired at us." Two more rockets landed nearby.

"No shit?" yelled Casey, pulling his head up from

between his knees. "Well, if we are goin' to be shelled like this, we should at least get some kind of record!"

With that, the others huddled in the trench began to yell. "Pour it on, motherfuckers! Fire some more, assholes! Is that all you got! Come on!"

O'Bryan couldn't believe what he was hearing. He thought, *mass hysteria.*

Finally, when O'Bryan began to wonder how long their luck could hold out in the trench. The shelling stopped. No one moved for a long time. The silence seemed deafening. Men began to stand up in the trench and shake loose dirt from themselves. It was getting dark now, and O'Bryan knew it would be another sleepless night. After the intense barrage, everyone would wait now for the other shoe to drop, the massive ground attack they all knew was coming.

"O'Bryan", the gunny's voice boomed out from the trench.

"Here, Gunny."

"All your people OK?"

"Everyone except Renarie. He's got some mosquito bites on his arm he wants a Purple Heart for."

"I been seriously wounded, Gunny!" yelled Renarie.

"Renarie, I don't think it would hurt you if you got hit with a two by four between the eyes."

"Hey, Gunny, you know I got feelings."

"Save it for the chaplain, Renarie. Captain says one hundred percent watch till further notice. No moon and fog tonight. Perfect night for them to come."

"Gunny!" yelled O' Bryan, "What was the count?"

"One thousand four hundred rounds of incoming according to the battalion count."

"That's a new record, ain't it, Gunny?"

"Yup, most rounds of incomin' by any one place so far in the war."

"Alright, we got the record!" yelled Casey.

O'Bryan interrupted, "Until tomorrow, anyway."

"Well, at least tomorrow we move into the new bunker," Casey added. "It'll be safer there."

Nguyen had watched the bombardment of Khe Sanh from a freshly dug trench line only 1200 meters west of the Marine base. He had reported to a captain who gave him food, water, and a new AK-47 rifle. His wounds were washed and bandaged by a young medic. The captain confirmed that Col. Linh was dead. Many other senior officers had been killed by American B-52 bombings near the division headquarters at Co Roc across the Laotian border.

"We still plan to carry out our mission here," the captain explained. "We have temporarily lost contact with division headquarters, but we still intend to carry on with the attack. I am very short of officers. Until further notice, you are now one of my company commanders."

"Thank you, sir," Nguyen replied.

"Your company is occupying the trench line to our east facing the Americans. Good luck."

Nguyen found his company in the trench line. The company consisted of only forty men. Many of these men were wounded in the Lang Vei attack. He hoped reinforcements would arrive soon. He had been told that more artillery and fresh men were on the way across the

Laotian border. Maybe the truck hauling the artillery would also bring mail. I must write a reply to Thi and send it back north with the returning trucks. At least she will know I am alive.

O'Bryan, Casey, and Renarie walked through the thick early morning fog to inspect the construction site of the super bunker. "I hope it's still there," Casey volunteered.

"Of course it is," said O'Bryan."

"We should finish it this morning," said Renarie.

All three men stopped at the edge of the new bunker and stared in disbelief. In the direct center of the bunker roof was a nice neat hole. The hole ran through two layers of steel runway matting.

"They sunk our fuckin' ark," Renarie blurted.

"Shit," said O'Bryan softly to himself.

They approached the steep ramp entrance and bent cautiously to peer inside. At the very bottom of the bunker was the four by six-foot inner bunker. Protruding from the bottom of this hole was the rear fin assembly of a Russian 122mm rocket.

"Dud?" asked Casey.

"Hope so," answered O'Bryan. "You know what this means?"

"What?" asked Renarie.

"Now, we got to fill in the bunker and bury the dud rocket."

"Shit," said Renarie, "we just finished diggin' it."

"Well, we will give it twenty-four hours, just in case it's got some type of delayed fuse. Just tell everyone to stay away from it."

"Look at the good side of this, Renarie," said Casey.

"What's that?"

"If we had worked a little harder and finished it, we all could have been in there when it hit."

Renarie began to laugh uncontrollably. Tears came to his eyes as he gasped for breath.

"What's so damned funny?" O'Bryan asked.

"I...I was just thinkin' about how they would have found all of us in there with that dud rocket. Our eyes bugged out, dead of heart attacks with our pants full of shit."

O'Bryan and Casey now began to laugh uncontrollably.

"Yup," said O'Bryan, "it would have been so stinky. They would have had to cover us all up, too."

Nguyen stood and gazed into the morning fog past the replacement troops filing by him to a trench which ran along the edge of a thick tree line. To the front of the trench was fifty meters of open ground. Beyond the open ground was an eight-foot-wide dirt road which ran from the Marine base at Khe Sanh to Route 9. This was a position between marines at Khe Sanh and Lang Vei where Col. Linh had planned to ambush any help coming to aid Lang Vei. The trench and adjacent bunkers were well concealed with foliage and dense brush. Even the loose dirt had all been removed. The fields of fire from the bunkers were interlocked and mutually supporting. It was a perfect death trap for any marines who ventured down the road.

Nguyen was jolted from his tactical gaze toward the dirt road by a familiar face crossing in front of him to the trench. "You there," he shouted. The young boy turned to face him. "Aren't you Hoan Lam from Thanh Hoa Province?"

"Yes, sir," Lam replied, stepping from the moving line of men.

Nguyen stepped forward to the young private. "I thought that was you. Do you recognize me?"

Hoan Lam looked at Nguyen with a blank stare.

Nguyen smiled, "My name is Vinh Nguyen. I remember you as only this high," he said, placing his hand palm down in front of his chest. "What are you doing here?"

A slow look of recognition crept across Lam's face. "Vinh Nguyen, yes, I remember you, sir. I have not seen you since," he paused, "since the bombs fell on us."

Nguyen turned away and beckoned Lam to follow him. After a few steps, he stopped and squatted to the ground. "Come and sit with me. I want to hear the news from home."

Lam squatted next to Nguyen, placing his AK-47 rifle on the ground, and was silent for a moment. He felt awkward being singled out by an officer. He remembered Nguyen, but they had not been friends. He was now seventeen, and Nguyen must have been at least twenty-four, an old man by his standards.

"You cannot be old enough to be here," Nguyen said, breaking the silence.

"I am seventeen, sir. I was drafted on my birthday six months ago."

"I thought you had to be eighteen to be drafted,"

Nguyen said, looking the boy next to him up and down.

"No, sir, that was changed. The country needs more men. The villages are emptying out. There are only old men, women, and children. Men leave, but no one comes back. The families don't know if their men are alive or dead. If a family doesn't receive mail from a soldier for a year, then they begin to think he is not coming home."

Nguyen was shocked to hear this. "You mean no one ever sends word to the families when our men die? We were told the political officers were taking care of notifying our families."

Hoan Lam sat silently and shook his head from side to side. In a low voice, he responded, "No one knows. I was told by a friend that the political cadres in the cities have lists of the dead, but they think it will be bad for the morale of the people to know so many have died." Lam paused and looked around to be sure he was not overheard. "There is also a rumor that many men who lost arms and legs are forced to stay in a special center in the highlands around Vinh Phuc. Again, so that their presence at home does not hurt the morale of the country."

"What?" yelled Nguyen, jumping to his feet. Hoan Lam remained squatting on the ground and lowered his head to his chest as if he personally bore the shame for this outrage.

Nguyen paced in front of Lam shaking his head up and down trying to vent his anger over these revelations.

"Surely, this can't be true," Nguyen said, more to himself than to his young friend. "I can understand that we hide our dead from our enemies but not from our own people!"

In a few minutes, he stopped pacing. His jaws ached

from being clenched. He looked down at the squatting head bowed figure of Hoan Lam and felt sorry for him.

"Hoan, I am not upset with you. I asked for the news, and you told me."

Hoan now stood and looked at Nguyen, his face visibly relieved.

"Lieutenant, is it true the war is nearly over? We were told in training that we control three-quarters of all the south. All we hear of is victory after victory."

Nguyen stopped and laughed out loud. "Little Private," he said, "look around you. We are in the extreme northwest tip of the south. We only control the ground we stand on. The war is far from over. You will learn soon not to believe everything the political cadre tell you. But enough about lies. How long did it take you to reach here from the north?"

"Forty-five days, Lieutenant," Hoan responded. "It was the worst experience of my life. We climbed the Truong Son and went days without food and sometimes even water. When we came out of the mountains, we were still 500 men strong, but on the thirtieth day, American bombs fell like rain from the sky with no warning. I was lucky. We were walking over a hill in a long column. Half of the column was in front of me. As I reached the top of the hill, the valley in front of me exploded with bombs, the whole valley! Two hundred men in front of me vanished in huge clouds of dirt. I dove to the ground but even the ground shook like an earthquake."

Nguyen reached out and put a hand on Lam's shoulder. The boy's eyes were wide with fear, but he continued recounting the experience.

"Hot pieces of dirt fell on me, and I couldn't breathe."

Lam suddenly fell silent, looking off in the distance. Nguyen knew the look. He had seen it on the face of many men who had seen sights beyond the endurance of the mind.

Now Lam continued in a soft voice, "We spent a day in that valley trying to find men and their equipment. We only found shreds of clothing and flesh along with some pieces of bent metal. It was as if the ground and the men became one. We could smell the dead but not see them. Fifty men deserted that night. In the morning, they were gone. I heard them talking. They said if the journey to the war was this bad, then the war itself must be truly terrible. Is the war more terrible than what I have seen?"

Nguyen looked Lam in the eye. "You have seen the death of your friends. You will see more. Why didn't you desert with the others?"

Lam's eyes narrowed. "I am no coward," he said pulling up the sleeve of his left arm to reveal a black ink tattoo. Nguyen turned his head sideways to read the lettering. He read, "Born in the North to Die in the South."

"If you remember, Lieutenant, my father was also killed in the village bombing by the Americans when your parents were killed. I could have hidden when the draft letter came. My mother told me to hide even though it meant our time would have been cut off by the village political office. But, I said no. I wanted to come to avenge my father. Even though the sons of party leaders leave to study overseas when they turn seventeen. They are cowards, not me."

"Private Lam, I am sure you are no coward. I am glad you made it to join us. Just be cautious. Listen to the older men who have been here awhile. They will keep you alive.

Now, go join your squad. It was good to see you."

"Yes, sir, thank you," Lam said picking up his weapon. He walked to the trench and dropped down inside. Nguyen's eyes followed his top half as Lam walked away and disappeared around a bend in the trench.

Born in the north to die in the south, Nguyen thought. He had seen that tattoo on many young replacements. For most of them, it had proven to be a fatal prophecy. He hoped that Lam's case might prove the exception.

So that is what it is like at home, he thought. *This war is bleeding my country to death.* He turned and called for his platoon sergeant. "Sergeant, send three men to relieve the observation post over the hill. It is time for those men to return and eat."

"Yes, sir," the Sergeant replied.

In a few minutes, he saw young Lam and two others climb from the trench and run forward across the open ground to disappear in the morning fog over a small rise. He turned to go to a freshly dug bunker which had become his new residence. Now, he thought, would be a good time to write Thi. Trucks had arrived carrying new artillery pieces yesterday. They had given the marines at Khe Sanh a good shelling. The fog was thick and that meant no American air strikes. The marines would not leave their bunkers and trenches to come out and fight today; visibility was too poor. He knew he must write a letter this morning in order to catch two of the trucks which were to carry wounded and mail back to the main army headquarters at Co Roc in Laos.

He wanted to ask Thi about the things Lam had told him, but he knew that censors read every letter before it was delivered. An indiscreet soldier's letter simply never arrived. He wondered often these days if all these rules were really for the good of the struggle or the good of the party officials. Knowledge, he had learned, was power. Manipulating information was how the party members stayed in power.

After looking up to see that the three relieved men had made it safely back, he sat in the doorway of his bunker. He reached back just inside his bunker and pulled his pack onto his lap. He retrieved some writing paper and a pen. He had only written, "Dear Thi," when he heard excited yelling coming from somewhere in the fog in front of the trench.

"The Americans are coming! The Americans are coming!" he heard. The cries sent adrenaline coursing through him. *You are an idiot*, he thought. *I should have known they would do what I least expected.*

Lam came running out of the fog first followed by two breathless comrades. "They're coming!" he gasped. "They're coming!"

Nguyen met Lam just behind the trench and grasped him by the shoulders with both hands. "Settle down. Settle down, Private. How many did you see?"

Lam caught his breath. "At least thirty or forty, maybe more. There could be many more following them. We didn't see them until they were on top of us because of the fog."

Nguyen turned to his sergeant, an older man who was nursing a leg wound and walked with a limp. "Sergeant, get every man to the trenches and bunkers. Break out extra machine gun ammunition and distribute it. I am going to the captain and ask for reinforcements to be sent. The Americans are bringing the battle to us."

Soldiers scurried in the tree-lined concealed trench as they worked to take up positions. Nguyen crouched low next to his kneeling radio operator trying to reach his captain on the radio.

"Tiger. Three to Tiger," he called, but there was no reply.

Suddenly, Nguyen saw reinforcements running low in the trees coming up behind him. Leading them was the captain who he was trying to reach on the radio. The captain ran to Nguyen and knelt beside him.

"No need to break radio silence, Lieutenant," he said. "We intercepted the American radio transmission at regimental headquarters. We knew the Americans were sending out patrols, but we just didn't know exactly where. Are your men ready?"

"Yes, sir," Nguyen replied. If they come following the men of our observation post, they will be dead center in our trap."

The Captain patted Nguyen on the shoulder then half turned facing him. "I will go take command of the men around the corner on the west side. You have the men here. Don't fire until they are in the killing zone." With that, he disappeared around the corner of the L-shaped trench.

Nguyen could hear American voices in the foggy distance. Then Nguyen saw them appear over a rise to his front, not even fifty meters from his trench. "Pass the word that there is to be no firing until the order is given," he whispered into the ears of the men on either side of him. Quietly, the word spread down the trench.

Nguyen watched with fascination as the American Marines formed a the line in the hazy distance. In the middle of the marines stood a man, obviously an officer, with a pistol over his head.

The Marine officer dropped his pistol, a sweeping movement downward, and the marines surged toward Nguyen's trench line. Nguyen was reminded of the charge made by the men of the young captain of the sapper's unit. *Very gallant,* he thought, *but doomed.*

The fog and thick trees kept Nguyen's men invisible until the marines were barely twenty meters away.

"Fire!" Nguyen commanded, and his entire section of the trench opened up. The volume of fire his men put out with their Ak-47s was incredible, one constant explosion. Screams and yells filled the air as the death struggles commenced.

The marines at first were surprised by the ambush. Nguyen saw one of the first marines go down shot in the head. The rifle fire being put onto the Americans was tearing the ground up. Large chunks of red clay were thrown in the air all around the marines.

Then the marines began to fight back blasting away at Nguyen and his men from less than twenty-five meters away. Bullets cracked past Nguyen's head, and two men next to him whirled down into the trench. Nguyen stopped his rifle to kneel and help them, but they were both dead, shot through the head. Blood, bone, and brain soaked into the red dirt.

He popped back up and saw an American standing in the middle of the battlefield, obviously shouting orders to his men. Nguyen was so close he could see the face of the American. He raised his AK-47 rifle to shoot the marine but froze as he caught sight of a hand grenade arching in the air just to his right. The grenade exploded in the trench ten feet away from him. The dust and dirt from the explosion filled the air and choked him as he drove left to the bottom of the trench. His left shoulder exploded in pain on impact from his bandaged wound, and he felt tiny fragments pierce his right arm and face. He lay there for a moment unable to hear and wondering if he was dead.

He sat up and spat dirt, half dazed. To his right were the mangled bodies of two men, one being his radio operator, who had absorbed most of the blast from the grenade. He looked up to see more of his fellow soldiers slipping over into the trench and beginning to fire.

Reinforcements, he thought. He looked down at his arm and saw tiny pinholes in his right arm sleeve. He knew his arm was bleeding, but he felt no pain. He found his rifle on the floor of the trench next to him and stood up quickly feeling a little dizzy. "Keep firing!" he yelled to his men, wiping a trickle of blood from his right eye.

A stream of bullets still cracked overhead and churned up geysers of dirt along the trench. Nguyen peeked over the top of the trench again, exposing only his head and arms, holding his rifle. His vision tunneled to the fight before him. Amazingly, the same American was still upright, now dragging a wounded man to a vacant stretch of trench to Nguyen's left front. Two bullets kicked dirt in Nguyen's face, and he dropped down into the safety of the trench. Then he heard the short end of the L-shaped trench, where the captain had gone, open fire. The combined fire now of over 100 men of the ambush filled the air and masked the screams and moaning of the wounded.

With fresh confidence from the additional rifle fire, Nguyen again raised to fire his weapon. The American was still there. *How can this be?* He now watched as the marine led three more wounded men back to the safety of the vacant trench. This time Nguyen sighted directly in the center of the marine who ran bent over back towards him. He squeezed the rifle trigger and simultaneously a nearby machine gun fired. The American fell, heavily riddled with bullets.

American mortar rounds began to hit behind Nguyen's trench. He heard cursing and crying from the wounded on the killing ground in front of him. A small group of Americans were shouting furiously as they retreated over the same small hill from where they had appeared. Nguyen saw them helping each other over the hill while others shot wildly back in his direction.

Then it was strangely quiet. Wounded and dead Americans littered the ground in front of him. A hazy, gray cloud drifted past the slaughter. The air smelled like gunpowder, fresh grass, and blood. Nguyen sat down heavily in the trench.

"Sergeant!" he yelled, standing up on wobbly legs.

"Here, sir," replied the old man with the limp.

"Find out how many wounded and dead we have."

"Yes, sir, but what about the enemy wounded?"

"Leave them for now."

The sergeant stepped over the bodies of the two dead men next to Nguyen and came to his side. "You are wounded yourself, Lieutenant. Sit down." Nguyen dropped heavily to the trench floor. The sergeant pulled a bandage from his cartridge belt carrier and wetted it. Then he began to dab blood from Nguyen's lacerated face. In the distance over the hill, more firing could be heard.

"It was a great victory, Lieutenant," the Sergeant said,

wiping blood from Nguyen's ear.

"We killed over half of them. Their bodies are scattered all over there," he said pointing to the killing zone.

"Yes, I know," Nguyen replied, smiling.

"I think I may have killed the bravest man I ever saw."

Nguyen caught a brief glimpse of something silver tumbling in the air over the sergeant's shoulder. The last thing he saw was a blinding yellow flash, and the sergeant disappeared. Then the world was scorching hot and black.

CHAPTER SEVENTEEN

The huge orange fireball sat over the distant brown hill like a sunset over a dirty sea. "Give it to 'em!" yelled Casey. "Burn the little fuckers up," chimed in Renarie.

Others cheered as O'Bryan stood next to the trench line while his squad below in the trench engaged in their favorite spectator sport, watching air strikes.

He had listened to Casey's radio all morning as the desperate men from the other platoon had pleaded for help and supporting fire. Now, the radio was ominously dead.

The whole company had watched for survivors of the patrol. Surviving marines struggled desperately over the barren, bombed-out brown terrain to return to the base. The enemy was concealed from view by tree lines and rolling hills. O'Bryan had raised his powerful ten-by-fifty binoculars once to view the early fighting. What he saw was too painful to bear, and he immediately dropped the binoculars where they hung now resting on his chest.

He and his men, along with the rest of the company, stood in full gear weighted down with rockets, grenades, and ammunition. They were locked and loaded just waiting for the word to rescue their fellow marines. Each man knew that it might be him out there next time. The 106mm recoilless refiles from the Ontos and fifty caliber machine guns on the west end perimeter had fired in support of the trapped platoon since some of the fighting was in direct sight of the base, but it was too late. Most of the men, from the sounds of the radio conversations, were killed in the first ten minutes of the fighting.

Another platoon from the company had been sent out the western gate down a dirt road which led to Route 9. They didn't get far before they were pinned down by heavy fire and in a fight for their lives, too.

O'Bryan's stomach churned. He swallowed down the copper taste of fear in the back of his mouth. *Thirty thousand North Vietnamese,* he thought, *that's what is out there. God knows how many are waiting for us.* He looked down at his assembled squad. They would all probably be dead by sunset. *I never thought I would survive this,* he thought. *Today is just as good a day as tomorrow to die. Maybe, I should write a letter to Susan and address it in case I don't come back. No, she has already had too much heartache from this war.* Strange, he really did matter to somebody. Somebody would cry if he died today. This knowledge, he knew, would make him a little more careful with his life.

"O'Bryan!" a deep voice yelled, pulling him back into reality. "Didn't you hear those mortars landing over by the airstrip?"

"No, Gunny," O'Bryan responded quickly. "There's always some kind of round impacting around here. That's a good forty yards away."

"Well, they could just as easy walk those 60mm mortar rounds right across here. Tell your men to stand down. We're not going out. The skipper was turned down by Battalion. We can't afford to lose any more men. You know the gooks will be waitin' for us to come for the bodies."

"But there might be some alive, Gunny."

"I know, I know, the skipper's sick about it, the lieutenant's sick about it, hell I'm sick about it. But we're Marines, and we follow orders."

"OK, Gunny," O'Bryan said in disgust.

He turned and knelt, then dropped into the trench next to the last man in his squad, who was Renarie. A loose shower of dirt followed him down.

"Pass the word people!" he yelled. "Stand down!"

"We ain't goin' out?" asked Renarie.

"Not today," O'Bryan replied.

"We just can't leave 'em out there," Renarie protested.

"Look, Renarie, they're dead. If they weren't dead before the airstrikes, they're dead now. Stand down! Those are the orders."

The men began to slowly file down the trench line to their bunkers. Casey remained behind looking at O'Bryan. His radio was slung over one shoulder, and his ridiculous one-lens black-framed glasses sat lopsided on his face. Casey took off his helmet and leaned against the trench. He shook his head.

"Poor bastards."

"I know," said O'Bryan. "But there will be plenty of time for payback."

"Payback's a motherfucker," Casey said, smiling.

"What kind of language is that from a good Catholic boy?" O'Bryan asked. "The sisters would be appalled."

Casey picked up his rifle, which had been leaning against the trench. "I don't think I'll ever be a good Catholic boy again. Not if I live through this."

Casey and O'Bryan began walking down the trench on the west side of the perimeter and had just reached the point where the trench curved back east on the south side. Suddenly, Pfc. Borden came tearing around the corner at full speed, nearly knocking Casey to the ground.

O'Bryan grabbed Borden's arm to keep him from

falling. Borden looked O'Bryan square in the face. Borden's eyes were wide with terror. In his right hand was a green C-Ration can.

"What's the matter?" O'Bryan demanded.

"He's coming!" exclaimed Borden breathlessly.

"All right, little fuck, here I come!" Renarie's voice boomed as he charged around the corner of the winding trench.

Borden escaped O'Bryan's grasp and ran full speed down the trench. Renarie appeared around the corner of the trench holding a square brown C-Ration box in his left hand. In his right hand, he held a machete, which he used for cutting jungle vines while on patrols.

"Hold it! Hold it!" yelled O'Bryan, grabbing Renarie's thick right arm, which held the machete in a death grip.

"You can't kill the little fuck."

Borden had stopped running now and slowly walked back towards O'Bryan, Renarie, and Casey. He stopped ten feet away from O'Bryan and Casey, who were both holding Renaire's massive arms.

"Can't kill me, you overgrown wop?" yelled Borden.

O'Bryan quickly responded, "Shut up, little fuck, before I let him go. They'll just say it was combat fatigue, and Casey and I will both swear Renarie was out of his head."

Casey smiled at Borden, "Yeah, I'll swear to it. Renaire just snapped."

"Where's your rifle?" O'Bryan yelled at Borden.

"Back in our bunker."

"You're supposed to have it with you all the time!" O'Bryan shouted back. Borden's eyes remained fixed on Renarie. "I didn't have time to get it, Corporal. The super wop was chasin' me."

"Go back and get your rifle, Borden. Renarie, give me the machete."

Renarie complied, handing O'Bryan the machete, handle first.

"What's all of this about, Renarie?" O'Bryan asked, still holding the big Italian's arm as Borden began to squeeze past them in the trench to return to his bunker.

Renarie's big brown eyes glared at Borden from under thick black brows. Renarie and Borden's faces were only inches apart as Borden squeezed past. Renarie spat his reply, "The little fuck stole my peaches and pound cake."

"Your peaches and pound cake?" asked O'Bryan.

"Yeah, got 'em right out of the C-ration box before I had a chance to open it."

"Well, what a little fuck," said Casey looking after Borden who was two steps away with his back to them.

"Borden," yelled O'Bryan. Borden stopped and spun around, fearing Renarie had escaped their squad leader. "You get the shitter detail tomorrow morning. What you did was as low as whale shit, so tomorrow morning you burn real shit."

"Come on, Corporal. You know the gook snipers always shoot at the guy who pulls the barrels out of 'em to burn 'em," pleaded Borden.

"Tough shit!" yelled Renarie, beaming his broadest Italian smile.

"Borden!" yelled O'Bryan holding up his right hand. "Give me."

Borden tossed the small cans of C-ration peaches and pound cake to O'Bryan. "Get out of here!" O'Bryan yelled. Borden turned to make his retreat.

O'Bryan turned to Renarie. "What's the matter with you?" he asked.

"He took my peaches and pound cake, Corporal."

"I know," replied O'Bryan. "But, you can't kill him for it."

"I wasn't goin' to kill him, Corporal, just cut him a little bit. You know, give him a scar to remember me by. You know, I really kind a like the little fuck."

"Well, we ain't got time for this shit, Renarie. Good men got killed out there today. Save your strength for the North Vietnamese." O'Bryan, Casey, and Renarie all turned to look towards the southwest where F-4 Phantom jets made steep bombing passes.

CHAPTER EIGHTEEN

No one talked about the dead marines. Some lying just beyond sight of the perimeter. It was a matter of shame and guilt. In conversations, they were referred to as "the lost patrol" or by the more superstitious as the "ghost patrol." There were orders from Saigon not to go after them and they had to be obeyed. O'Bryan and his men continued their daily routines and waited. They cleaned their weapons, wrote letters home and waited some more. They suffered more incoming rocket and artillery fire and waited. Finally, three weeks after the patrol they got the word.

"O'Bryan," yelled the gunny, working his way down the trench past other squad members cleaning their rifles.

"Here, Gunny," replied O'Bryan, looking up from where he sat with his M16 on his lap.

"You marines get those weapons good and clean," the gunny announced to everyone. "You are going to need them in the morning. Tape down anything that makes a noise. No canteen cups. Stuff some rags in around your cleaning gear. Tape your dog tags. We want to be silent and deadly in the morning. O'Bryan, you come with me to the platoon C.P. bunker for a squad leaders meeting. The rest of you men get busy. It's payback time."

"You heard the gunny," O'Bryan yelled, snapping the two halves of his broken down M16 back together. He rose to follow the gunny back down to the platoon C.P. bunker. He walked past Casey, smiling. "Payback's a motherfucker," he said, walking away without looking back.

The morning was dark and the damp air formed a fine mist. The procession of marines moved in a single file to staging areas along the perimeter's western trench line. O'Bryan learned at the squad leaders meeting that he would be an extra forward observer on the patrol. Casey would be his radio operator. Renarie would lead O'Bryan's squad.

The usual joking and cursing complaints which accompanied the movement of the marines were absent. O'Bryan took his place in line with the second platoon C.P. group followed by Casey with his radio. An officer Forward Observer Team would travel with the Company Command Post Group. If one group was wiped out then the other group could call in supporting fire. *Everyone's expendable,* thought O'Bryan.

When the line of men stopped moving down the trench line everyone stopped and sat down in place. O'Bryan relaxed and leaned back against the dirt wall of the six-foot-deep trench. He felt safe in the darkness. The night was now his old friend.

Soon the sun began to rise and infused the thick fog with an eerie subdued glow. Visibility was only four to six feet. O'Bryan closed his eyes and heard his heart pounding.

In a moment he and Casey began to rise with the other marines in the trench line staging area. They all began to make last minute checks of weapons and equipment. Casey looked at O'Bryan and pushed his one lens black-framed glasses back on his nose. He bent forward and whispered with a smile to O'Bryan, "Ask not what your country can do for you."

O'Bryan nodded and smiled back, "They shot him too

you know." The smiles quickly vanished. O'Bryan knew this was a sacred mission. An unwritten contract he and all marines had with dead brothers. *We are coming for you,* he thought. *We always come for our own. How many of us will join you today?*

As they moved out, O'Bryan realized the plastic-encased map he carried was useless in the thick white shroud of fog. Until it cleared no one could call in or adjust supporting fire. No one could say with absolute certainty where they were located on the map, much less see impacting artillery or mortar fire to make adjustments.

Of course, this is a two-edged sword, O'Bryan thought. It also gave them perfect cover as they advanced on the North Vietnamese positions. No one would see them coming. The fight would be at close quarter and the knew all the marines longed to shoot an N.V.A. after weeks of shelling.

O'Bryan watched the ground in front of him as the company slowly moved forward. At first he counted his steps trying to determine how far they had advanced from their own wire. All he could see was the faint dark outline of the man in front of him in the swirling white fog. Soon he lost track of the number of steps. He kept waiting for the sonic crack of AK-47 rifles to pierce the white goop with green tracer bullets.

Suddenly, artillery from behind him boomed. The big rounds swooshed overhead and landed with thunderous red glowing cracks in the fog ahead. O'Bryan knew these were the preplanned artillery covering fires, but instinctively his knees still buckled at the sound of them. At first, the artillery explosions were close ahead. Then they began to move further away. O'Bryan's stomach fluttered. He knew the first barrage was plotted on the closest enemy trench line. Soon they would be on top of them.

The fog began to gradually lift and exposed more marines in front and behind him. They crossed a small dirt road that he knew was about 200 meters from the wire and led from the base to Route 9.

He went over a small rise and then stopped abruptly. In front of him was a trench line. *We are on top of the North Vietnamese and so far not a shot fired,* he thought. A marine in front of O'Bryan turned and motioned up and down with an outstretched hand. O'Bryan and Casey sat down in place. In a few moments the marine in front of O'Bryan stood up and waved them forward. The fog was still thick and low to the ground along the North Vietnamese trench. They moved forward, stepping softly across the trench.

Once across, the sit signal was given again and they went down on some freshly dug dirt. He and Casey sat back to back. The rush of his own blood roared in O'Bryan's ears. The total silence served to enhance the unreal quality of the whole morning as the marines waited in the witches' brew.

Slowly, nearly imperceptibly, the fog began to lift. Now O'Bryan could see ten feet, then twenty feet. The white blanket peeled back and revealed the fresh earth they were sitting on was the top of a North Vietnamese bunker. The trench line they had stepped across snaked its way left and right connecting other bunkers, then disappeared in the white mist. O'Bryan looked to his right. As far as he could see in the fog, marines sat atop the enemy trench line. Where, he asked himself, were the North Vietnamese?

O'Bryan looked down into the trench line and saw many sets of fresh boot prints in the wet red clay. A delicious warmth began to spread over him as he realized the answer to his own question. The North Vietnamese were inside their bunkers and holes along the trench line. Somehow the marines had walked in and sat down on top of them without even as much as alerting an N.V.A. listening post. *This is so sweet,* he thought.

Then he heard the trickling of dirt below him in the trench line. A young North Vietnamese soldier crawled on all fours out of a small hole in the side wall of the trench. The hole was the entrance to the bunker he and Casey sat upon.

O'Bryan slowly raised his M16 and aligned the front sight blade on the middle of a shiny mass of black hair, which was the back of the soldier's head. For some reason he did not understand, he hesitated pulling the trigger.

He watched, fascinated as the young man stood upright in the trench and stretched, arms to his side on his tiptoes. In one outstretched hand the soldier held a softball sized ball of rice. In the other hand O'Bryan saw a set of metal tongs and a small metal bowl. On that arm, O'Bryan noted some sort of tattoo with some sort of Vietnamese writing. *He's about to have breakfast,* O'Bryan thought. O'Bryan felt as if he were invisible and wondered how long he could watch the young boy before he had to kill him.

As if to answer the question, artillery from Khe Sanh began to fire again. The North Vietnamese soldier squatted instinctively as the rounds passed overhead. He turned wide-eyed and faced O'Bryan who pulled the trigger and fired a bullet through the young soldier's forehead.

O'Bryan felt Casey jump as he fired two more times

into the North Vietnamese who grabbed his head, screamed, then sat down heavily in the trench. The rice, tongs and bowl fell silently to the ground.

O'Bryan and Casey dropped quickly into the trench line landing on either side of a bunker entrance. They could hear panicky tones of North Vietnamese voices inside the bunker.

O'Bryan pulled a round M33 hand grenade from his big jungle utilities side leg pocket and motioned for Casey to do the same. O'Bryan quickly leaned his rifle against the trench wall, pulled the grenade pin, let the spoon fly, hesitating a second before throwing the grenade into the bunker entrance hole. Casey's grenade followed O'Bryan's and two seconds later there was a muffled explosion which blew screams, dirt and smoke out the bunker entrance into the trench. O'Bryan looked across the billowing dirt cloud and saw Casey bending to find his glasses on the ground.

O'Bryan stepped in front of the round hole that was the entrance. In the dim light and swirling dust inside he saw two N.V.A. lying on the bunker floor, moaning. He fired two rounds into the head of each wounded soldier, then stepped away from the entrance.

"Are they still alive?" Casey asked, fumbling to put his glasses back on.

"Not anymore," replied O'Bryan. "Come on, let's check the rest of the holes in this section of the trench." One by one he and Casey began to check the holes in the side of the trench for enemy occupants. There were several down the line, however, they were all empty.

The gunny dropped down into the trench next to Casey. "What you got, O'Bryan?"

"Not much, Gunny. I think we caught a listening post asleep. We killed all three of 'em. No one else seems to be at home here."

"Good work," said the gunny, surveying the dead North Vietnamese soldier in the trench. The gunny bent down and held up the dead boy's arm.

"See this tattoo?"

"Yeah," replied O'Bryan.

"I read an intelligence flyer from down south about North Vietnamese infiltrators. This says, 'Born in the North to Die in the South.'"

O'Bryan smiled. "Glad we could help make his wish come true."

"Jesus," said Casey, "This is just a kid."

"Young ones will kill you just as dead as old ones," the gunny replied, looking around the trench. The gunny looked in the bunker entrance at the two bodies. "I hope they didn't have a chance to warn anyone that we're coming."

"I don't think so," said O'Bryan, changing magazines on his M16.

"Well you and Casey get back up on the bunker and keep your eyes peeled. The company will assault from this trench line in five minutes towards hill 471. I don't think the N.V.A. have a clue we're out here yet." With that, the gunny began to move down the trench to place other marines where he wanted them.

The fog was completely gone now and O'Bryan could see that the trench extended to the southwest towards the rolling ground at the base of hill 471. He knew from the briefing that the base of hill 471, or 600 meters, was the ultimate limit of the Marine advance today.

The men from the rest of the company began to arrive along with the Company Command Post Group. O'Bryan knew the plan. Wipe out any resistance where he was at, then take the first objective 'Alpha' at the base of hill 471.The rest of the company would provide cover while search teams would recover bodies from the lost patrol. O'Bryan thought it sounded like a good plan. He also knew from experience that battle plans only survived until the first shots. He lay on the sandbagged roof of the bunker, studying the ground between them and hill 471 with his field glasses. So far he could see no sign of movement, only reddish brown bomb-scarred earth and thick brush.

Casey lay next to O'Bryan, prone on the bunker. The PRC-25 radio he carried was shoved deep down into his green marine backpack on his back. The antenna of the radio was bent double and placed down the side of the radio inside the pack. The radio handset was hidden in his jungle utilities breast pocket under his bulky dirty green flak jacket. O'Bryan had told Casey that if he could tell that Casey was carrying a radio he would kick his butt. Casey knew the threat was reasonable. If the North Vietnamese could tell he was carrying a radio then he and anyone close to him would become a prime enemy target.

Casey rolled to one side and squinted at O'Bryan next to him "O'Bryan?"

"What?"

"Look at me again and see if you can tell I'm wearin' a radio."

O'Bryan lay on his stomach with his elbows propping binoculars to his eyes. Without looking away from the field glasses he replied, "I looked at it once already, Casey."

"Just one more time," said Casey rolling to his

stomach.

"Nope, can't see any part of the radio," O'Bryan replied.

"Good," said Casey, rolling back to his right side.

O'Bryan picked up the binoculars and began study some 105mm and 155mm Marine artillery impacting 600 meters to their front. He turned to Casey, "I think there's some more trenches out there but I can't see anybody movin' around in 'em, though."

Casey rolled to his left side and fished a C-ration pack of five cigarettes from his right breast pocket. He lit a cigarette and offered one to O'Bryan.

"No thanks," said O'Bryan.

Casey lay looking at O'Bryan a moment. "What all kinds of shit are you carryin'?"

O'Bryan answered without putting the binoculars down from his eyes. "Two ammo bandoliers with thirty-two loaded M16 magazines, a spare M79 grenade launcher I dug up, one bandolier of high-explosive rounds and one bandolier of beehive rounds for the 79. Three M33 grenades, a .45 in a shoulder holster and this L.A.W. rocket across my back."

Casey studied O'Bryan for a moment. "All I got is eight loaded magazines for my M16 and three M33s."

"Well, if I get killed," O'Bryan said matter-of-factly, "you can strip this stuff off me and use it. Don't let 'em capture you."

"Thanks," Casey said, "that makes me feel much better."

"Fix bayonets!" a command echoed to their left. O'Bryan turned to see the other two platoons of the company preparing to cross the trench to the left rear. The men who had them all reached and drew bayonets from their scabbards, which mostly hung from webbed cartridge belts. The clicking noise of the bayonets being attached to rifle barrels filled the air as over a hundred marines fixed bayonets. Chills went down O'Bryan's back. He had seen this in old World War II movies, but he never thought he would see the real thing, much less be part of it.

"Shit," Casey said, "this is much too serious."

The marines moved out, walking past O'Bryan and the rest of his platoon, who stayed put along the trench as a reserve force. The marines spread out in long squad formations to form wedges and echelons left and right.

O'Bryan had been studying the ground they were crossing. It was mostly barren. Red rolling hills were pockmarked by intense bombing with large craters that littered the open ground. He watched as the company C.P. group peeled off into a big shell crater to direct the coming fight. Behind him, in another shell crater, was a navy doctor and several corpsmen in a makeshift triage center. O'Bryan turned around and watched the marines advance to his front. "Get ready," he said to Casey. "The shit is about to hit the fan."

Casey moved to a sitting position next to O'Bryan. "You know, O'Bryan, if you didn't know better you would swear this is World War I."

Artillery shells in the distance to the front of the advancing marines creating one huge cloud of expanding reddish brown dust. The advancing lines of marines disappeared into the billowing dust.

O'Bryan checked his map to see what contour lines lay under the bombardment. He knew that soon the artillery would have to lift as the marines drew closer to the N.V.A. positions. Then the real fight would start.

The dust cleared and O'Bryan watched through his binoculars as marines assaulted across the open ground with fixed bayonets on line. The advance was slow with men looking left and right to stay on line. Puffs of brown smoke marked enemy 60mm mortar rounds which began to fall around the advancing men, but no one faltered. The advancing line ground on. More artillery from Khe Sanh swooshed overhead and landed in the distance, silencing the enemy mortars.

As the marines crossed a low hill, O'Bryan heard the cracks of what had to be hundreds of AK-47 rifles and enemy machine guns opening fire. Stray bullets cracked and whizzed over his and Casey's heads. O'Bryan watched through the field glasses, prone on the N.V.A. bunker roof. He saw fellow marines being hit and corpsmen running under fire to treat them. The advancing marines had halted and were down on the ground. More artillery from Khe Sanh flew overhead impacting close to the distant line of marines. He could see marines on the ground pouring fire into North Vietnamese trenches and bunkers. Hand grenades sailed back and forth mixed with larger 82mm mortar rounds from N.V.A. tubes that began to explode among the attacking marines. O'Bryan watched with admiration as three- and four-man teams of marines ran under fire and disappeared into enemy trenches. Suddenly there were explosions along the enemy trench line and mutually supporting bunkers. He saw one marine stand with a flame thrower, then spray a stream of fire into an unseen bunker. It looked to O'Bryan that he and Casey, along with the other men of the reserve platoon might not be needed.

He put down his field glasses then held them out to Casey. "Take a look. It's great. We are kicking their ass," he said smiling.

Casey put the binoculars to his eyes. He had patiently waited to see what was happening in front of them. Casey looked and struggled to make some sense of what appeared to be complete chaos in front of him.

O'Bryan lay motionless, watching the fight. He looked to his left front at the shell crater holding the C.P. Group. Suddenly, explosions erupted as N.V.A. 82mm mortar rounds showered the hole and surrounding area. Thick red dust boiled from the crater. It appeared to O'Bryan that the whole Command Post Group must be dead. At the same time the volume of fire increased on the assaulting force of marines. "Counterattack," he mumbled to himself.

"What?" Casey asked.

"Nothing, just stay here. I got to go find Mr. Henderson." O'Bryan rose to a squatting position. He spotted Lt. Henderson on the floor of the trench line behind him. He leapt into the trench and ran past other marines to Henderson who was squatted down next to his radio operator who sat on the dirt floor.

"Lieutenant!" O'Bryan yelled breathlessly. "They got the whole C.P. Group, mortars, direct hit."

Lt. Henderson knelt over his radio operator and without looking up replied, "I know. I saw it. I am trying to raise someone on the radio now."

The young radio operator continued to call the C.P. group without an answer. "No good, Mr. Henderson."

"That's it!" the lieutenant said, whirling around to O'Bryan. "If those two platoons stay in the open ground around the N.V.A. bunkers much longer they will be wiped out."

"Lieutenant," the radio operator interrupted, "they are both pinned down and are reporting heavy casualties."

Henderson turned to O'Bryan. "Tell the gunny to get everybody up and ready. We got to take the high ground above where our people are out there or they're all dead. Move!"

O'Bryan raced down to the other end of the trench. "Gunny!" he yelled. "Henderson says get everybody up. We gotta go help First and Third Platoons."

The gunny's voice boomed over the noise of the battle. "Platoon, saddle up, we are goin' to kick some ass."

The whole platoon formed along the captured enemy trench. Lt. Henderson turned to the gunny. "You stay here with third squad. Watch out for Doc and the corpsmen in the shell hole with the wounded. First and second squads come with me. O'Bryan!"

"Yes, sir?"

"You are now second squad leader again."

"Got it," O'Bryan snapped back.

Renarie, who stood next to Casey, ten feet away from Lt. Henderson, wrinkled his nose and furrowed his bushy black eyebrows. "Big fuckin' deal," he commented to Casey. "So he's gonna be squad leader instead of me. We are all probably gonna fuckin' die anyway."

The two squads moved out from the safety of the trench line, the lieutenant with first squad and O'Bryan following with second squad.

Immediately, bullets cracked overhead and sent up small puffs of red dust in the dirt around them. O'Bryan led his squad and followed in trace of the lieutenant and first squad. O'Bryan's vision began to narrow to his immediate front. North Vietnamese popped up from trenches and fired at nearby marines in bomb craters.

From shell hole to shell hole, the two squad swiftly moved across the hundred meters of open ground. They took turns firing cover fire for each other during the short frantic spurts.

O'Bryan had nearly reached the safety of a shell hole at a dead run, bent as low to the ground as he could go. His M16 dangled from his right hand. The red dirt to his front exploded with the impact of AK-47 rounds. *Running is too slow,* he thought, and dove the last four feet headfirst into a bomb crater. He landed on three dead North Vietnamese soldiers. Brain matter oozed from the head wound of one N.V.A. who lay face down clawing the red dirt with his right hand next to O'Bryan.

He rolled off the dead N.V.A. soldier and crawled up to the lip of the ten-foot-wide shell crater. To his right he saw Casey dive into an adjacent crater. Ducking and diving at five- to ten-meter intervals, the rest of the fourteen-man squad followed. O'Bryan spotted dust kicking up from a firing port fifty meters to his front in an N.V.A. bunker. He sighted his rifle on the small black opening and squeezed off five quick rounds. In reply, a torrent of bullets cracked over his head from an unseen AK-47, forcing him lower in the crater. He turned to count his men. Amazingly they were all there, including Casey, who crawled up next to him.

"The lieutenant wants you, O'Bryan," Casey said, handing O'Bryan the radio handset.

"Go ahead to Bravo 2-2," O'Bryan said into the hand set.

"Get your people ready to cover us. We are going to the next crater forty meters to your right front. You occupy the one we are in now after we get there. We'll give you covering fire, over."

"Bravo 2-2 clear and out," O'Bryan answered. He handed the handset back to Casey then yelled behind him to the other squad members. "Get your asses up on the rim and give first squad covering fire." The squad responded, each man crawling to the rim of the crater to form a semicircle of fire.

O'Bryan pulled off his helmet and unslung the M79 grenade launcher, which had been across his back. He pulled four high-explosive rounds from a bandolier slung across his flak jacket. He also unslung the L.A.W. rocket which had been across his back and handed it to Casey. "Make sure none of our people are behind you when you fire this."

Casey reached up from his prone position, took the disposable green 66mm rocket. "Thanks," he said, squinting at O'Bryan through his one good eyeglass lens.

Moans and curses from nearby wounded men filled the air, mixed with rifle fire and exploding mortar rounds. O'Bryan was oblivious to the chaotic sounds, concentrating on his task. He yelled over his shoulder to the others in the squad. "First left, then right. I'll mark the targets with the M79. Shoot where you see my rounds hit or anywhere you see a gook." He turned to Casey. "Tell the L.T. we are ready."

In a moment, Casey looked up at O'Bryan, nodded and yelled, "Open fire!"

O'Bryan raised and fired an M79 round at a nearby enemy bunker. The whole squad fired at the bunker and trench line, which extended to another bunker. Bullets whipped the dirt around the target bunker and set off a frenzy of small brown eruptions. He quickly reloaded the M79 and fired at an adjacent enemy bunker, which shifted the squad's fire from his first target. He saw movement to his left front and turned to watch the lieutenant and first squad charge across open ground slightly uphill from them. "Keep shooting," he yelled to the rest of his squad. "Pour it on!" He raised his M79 and fired, then reloaded and fired again and again in rapid succession as the lieutenant and first squad disappeared uphill into another trench line.

O'Bryan sat up just below the rim of the bomb crater. "Cease fire, cease fire!" he yelled. "Get those satchel charges ready. We're going across to link up with first squad. Casey, you stay right behind me. Keep at least a ten-meter interval. If I yell for the radio come up next to me. Otherwise ten meters behind me."

"Got it," Casey said while pulling pins from an L.A.W. rocket he carried.

O'Bryan raised his arm and motioned everyone forward, "Second squad on line! Go! Go!" The whole squad arose as one man from the shell crater and quickly spread on line parallel to the N.V.A. trench in front of them. They were moving at a dead run firing rifles and machine guns from the hip. Some were tossing hand grenades as they ran.

O'Bryan paused, looking back to check Casey when a round cracked over his head. He instinctively turned and dove for the ground in one motion. For a fraction of a second he saw a North Vietnamese soldier in a green shirt rise up from the trench line thirty meters to his direct front.

Suddenly he felt as if someone had hit the side of his helmet with a baseball bat. For a moment everything went black. His helmet went flying and the thunderous thud of a bullet striking steel filled his ears. His eyes opened and he knew he was alive. To his front, as if in slow motion, he saw the same N.V.A. soldier rise, taking careful aim. He tried to move but seemed unable to lift his arms. He closed his eyes and waited for the AK-47 bullet to hit him.

Instead, he heard a large explosion. He opened his eyes and saw only smoke and a red dirt cloud where the N.V.A. had been. Casey crawled up next to him, dragging an empty plastic L.A.W. rocket tube behind him.

"You hit, O'Bryan?"

"I don't know. Is the back of my head OK?"

Casey inspected O'Bryan's head on one elbow. "Looks OK to me."

O'Bryan felt his arms tingling. He moved one leg, then the other. He made a fist with his left and then right hand. He reached up and patted his head. "Where's my helmet?" he asked Casey.

"I'm not sure," Casey replied. "I saw the gook shoot and your helmet flew off as you were going down. Heard it hit your helmet. Thought you were dead."

"What happened to the gook?"

Casey drug the expended plastic rocket tube up next to him. "Got him with this thing. Hit him right in the chest and he kind of disappeared." Casey held up the spent plastic tube. "Do we save these?"

O'Bryan shook his head, "No dipshit, they're disposable. Just like us."

Two 60mm mortar rounds impacted close by them.

"Let's go," O'Bryan yelled to Casey. "I can run now. Head for the trench. Catch up with the rest of the squad."

O'Bryan grabbed his M16 rifle, which lay next to him and they jumped to a running crouch to cover the open ground to the enemy trench. He noticed there was no enemy fire as they quickly dropped into the N.V.A. trench line.

Up and down the trench line O'Bryan and Casey saw marines moving methodically from hole to bunker to hole as if they had been choreographed to achieve deadly precision. Some were using shaped satchel charges while others threw grenades. There were secondary explosions in some of the bunkers as North Vietnamese ammunition exploded.

O'Bryan heard Renarie's thick Boston accent, "Good mornin', motherfuckers!" followed by a muffled explosion to his left. The killing frenzy in the trench went on and on. There was little return fire from the North Vietnamese. O'Bryan and Casey knelt down in the trench for a quick breather and looked around.

Casey looked carefully at O'Bryan. "You sure you're OK, Corporal?"

"Sure, Casey, I'm fine. Keep an eye out. The N.V.A. may counterattack."

Casey turned his head to peer over the trench line to their front. "There's not that many of us out here. You think we got our bodies back?"

"Don't know, Casey, but I can tell you we sure made some new ones," O'Bryan replied, glancing around at North Vietnamese bodies sprawled on the trench floor. O'Bryan took out a plastic canteen and took a big gulp. He offered the canteen to Casey who turned it down with a sideways nod.

Casey looked at a dead North Vietnamese soldier lying three feet away. The body lay on its side in a doubled up fetal position. Blood pooled under the chest and there were three bullet holes stitched across the back of his green shirt. An AK-47 rifle lay next to him. Casey looked to O'Bryan, "Think we're winning?"

O'Bryan smiled, "We're winning," he said pointing to the dead body. "He lost. By the way, good shot with the rocket or else I would be one of the losers today."

"Think nothing of it. Beginner's luck."

"I know," O'Bryan paused, "that's what's so fucking scary!"

O'Bryan and Casey both began to laugh uncontrollably. Tears came to O'Bryan's eyes and left streaks of red dirt on his face. Casey was forced to remove his one-lens pair of glasses to wipe tears from his right eye.

The radio handset crackled with a voice from under Casey's flak jacket. The laughing spasm was over as quickly as it had begun. Casey put his glasses back on and pulled the radio handset from beneath his jacket.

"Bravo 2-2 go," he said, squeezing the long black transmitter switch on the side of the handset. "Wait one," Casey said, handing the handset O'Bryan. The lieutenant's voice boomed into O'Bryan's ear, "Get your men ready. We are going to pull out of here before the N.V.A. counterattack, over."

"Bravo 2-2 clear, out," replied O'Bryan. He turned to Renarie. "Get everybody ready, we are fuckin' gettin' outta here. We got anybody can't walk?"

Renarie looked at the exhausted squad, "No, all these

motherfuckers are not only walking, just give the word and we can fly."

O'Bryan stood for a quick look then went down on one knee facing his men down the trench line, "We go out same way we came in here. We are playin' leap frog with first squad again. This time we go backwards. Get in position to give covering fire."

The squad members all faced west in the trench toward a tree line at the very crest of the gradual hillside they occupied. O'Bryan judged the distance to the tree line at no more than thirty meters. He broke open his M79 grenade launcher and inserted an HE round. He laid two more rounds next to his feet on the trench floor for quick reloading.

Casey knelt next to O'Bryan in the trench waiting for the word from the lieutenant. His radio handset spat out the words, "Bravo 2-2 this is Bravo Actual, open fire!"

O'Bryan sighted the M79 on the middle of the tree line and yelled, "Open fire!" He fired the grenade launcher and quickly reloaded. To his left he saw the lieutenant with first squad pulling back to another abandoned enemy trench. O'Bryan's squad continued to pour fire into the tree line while receiving little or no return fire.

Casey leaned up and at O'Bryan's ear, "Two actual says its our turn now."

"Cease fire, cease fire," O'Bryan yelled to his squad. "Saddle up, we are movin' back next." The squad began to collect ammunition and any other weapons in preparation for the withdrawal to the next trench behind them. O'Bryan was adjusting the PRC 25 radio in the pack on Casey's back when he heard Renarie scream.

"Holy fuck, here they come."

O'Bryan turned in the trench to see the tree line southwest of them come alive with N.V.A. The troops in green uniforms and helmets surged over the hilltop and down toward O'Bryan's men in the trench.

Renarie's machine gun opened up in thirty-round bursts. The air was once again full of sonic cracks and rifle reports punctuated by O'Bryan's M79 rounds exploding.

Suddenly, an N.V.A. .51-caliber machine gun began to fire at them from the tree line. Huge chunks of red dirt flew into the air as the rounds impacted around them.

"Get down! Get down!" O'Bryan yelled as the big gun swept the trench his men occupied. Huge chunks of red dirt flew into the air as the .51-caliber rounds impacted around them.

O'Bryan reached for the radio handset as he and Casey huddled next to each other on the floor of the N.V.A. trench.

"Bravo 2, Bravo 2, this is Bravo 2-2, over," O'Bryan yelled into the handset. "Lieutenant, we got about a hundred black hats with a heavy machine gun to our right front. We are in a world of shit if we don't get some kind of supporting fire, over."

The lieutenant's voice came back quickly, "Bravo 2-2, have your people throw grenades. Have one of them throw a smoke to mark your extreme left front. Then get everybody down. This will be close."

"Roger that and out," O'Bryan replied. He then peeked over the top of the trench and saw scores of North Vietnamese advancing from the tree line to his left front. He turned and yelled down the trench line. "Everybody get a grenade ready and throw when I give the word then get down." He pulled a green smoke grenade from his belt suspender straps where it had been held with black tape. He held the grenade in his right hand with three fingers over the long spoon. He pulled the pin. "Throw grenades!" he yelled and heaved the green smoke to the edge of his position.

The rest of the squad simultaneously pitched their M33 grenades at the advancing N.V.A. AK-47 rifle fire popped over the trench. Green tracers flew over O'Bryan's and Casey's heads as the explosions from the grenades filled the air with red dust. The enemy .51-caliber machine gun opened up again, this time from nearer in the tree line. The squad lay flattened at the bottom of the four-foot trench. Casey turned and yelled into O'Bryan's ear, "We're fucked."

Two red tracers accompanied by a heavy cracking noise flew overhead to the left front of the marines. O'Bryan turned his head and smiled at Casey as he shoved on top of Casey's helmet, forcing his face in the dirt.

Two huge explosions erupted to the left front of the trench line in the middle of the advancing North Vietnamese troops. They were quickly followed by three more explosions. Dirt and parts of bodies rained along the hillside. Before the debris could all fall back, three more explosions tore into the tree line where the N.V.A. had emerged. Suddenly the battlefield was strangely silent. O'Bryan's ears rang as a red dirt cloud smelling of cordite and burnt tissue drifted over them.

The radio handset crackled with a voice. Casey took the handset and handed it to O'Bryan. "Bravo 2-2, this is Bravo Actual, any casualties, over?"

"Two Actual this is 2-2, negative. That was some shooting by those 106s, over."

"That was some of the Ontos firing all the way from the base. Get your people out of there, we are pulling back, over."

"We are on the way Two Actual," replied O'Bryan. He handed the radio handset back to Casey and rose from one knee to a crouched standing position. "Everyone out of here but Renarie and Mike with the machine gun. We'll cover them while they fall back. Let's go, second squad, we are gettin' out of here. Get a move on before the assholes get more mortars set up."

Chapter Nineteen

That afternoon, O'Bryan and Casey sat inside O'Bryan's bunker cleaning their weapons. O'Bryan sat legs crossed with his M16 spread out on a green towel on the dirt floor. Casey sat across from O'Bryan cleaning the M79 with a bottle of cleaning solvent and a tooth brush. Casey looked up from the M79. "I can't believe no one in our squad was hit. I mean how lucky was that?"

"I know," O'Bryan replied. "I told you I was good luck."

"Well, maybe so but I think you used up a lot of that when that N.V.A. shot off your helmet. What was the last word on our casualties?"

O'Bryan worked on the face of the M16 bolt with a toothbrush. He looked up and a furrow of concern creased his forehead. "We lost twelve, killed, and fifty wounded from the company."

"How many N.V.A. we get?" asked Casey.

"Word is the aerial observers spotted 115 dead N.V.A. on the ground and probably more in the bunkers they couldn't see."

"Mail call," Gunny Timmons's face appeared bent over in the bunker doorway. He threw a letter and a magazine to O'Bryan. "Nothin' for you today, Casey," Timmons said, quickly moving away, his voice shouting "Mail call!" as he moved down the trench.

O'Bryan looked at the letter on his lap. It was from Susan Williams. He unconsciously caught his breath. He reached down and took the just-delivered *Time* magazine and handed it to Casey. Casey accepted the magazine in his right hand. He looked at the letter on O'Bryan's lap.

"Thanks," Casey said. "I hope that's not a Dear John letter."

O'Bryan raised his eyebrows. "Asshole, all my letters are Dear John letters. It's my name."

"Oh yeah, I forgot that is your name. Seems like in the Marines nobody has a first name." Casey wrapped a green towel around the freshly cleaned M79. He picked up the magazine and started for the bunker entrance. "I'm going retire to a more private location to read my new *Time* magazine. Looks like some more stuff in here about us at Khe Sanh."

O'Bryan snapped the two parts of his M16 back together and looked up at Casey. "Stay low, and run over there and back. The sniper hasn't shot at anyone going to the head today. You're safe once you get inside."

Casey adjusted his glasses as he emerged from the bunker. He jumped out of the trench and ran a zig zag pattern to the small sandbagged wooden shack. Once inside, he seated himself on the two-holer. The smell of diesel fuel and burnt excrement was overwhelming as he tried to hold his breath. His eyes adjusted to the dim light and he bent sideways trying to make out some graffiti on the wall next to him. Some of it was standard stuff. "Eat the apple, fuck the corps," a globe and anchor with "Simply Forgot Us," inscribed below. Then in bold strokes, "I think I love Fred." Casey laughed deep and long in the foul air. He then opened the new *Time* magazine to an article on Khe Sanh.

O'Bryan took his flak jacket off and placed it on the side of the trench. He climbed up on the trench side and sat next to the flak jacket. Finally, he opened the letter from Susan Williams and began to read in the fading light.

Dear John,

I have changed my mind. It's one o'clock in the morning, and I want a letter from you. I had dinner tonight with Tom Parkhurst (you remember the law student that I was dating). Well, it seems he asked me to marry him. Of course, I said, "no!" Then I told him I was in love with you. He didn't take it well. He asked me what kind of a future I could possibly have with a dumb Marine who was probably already dead. I told him that you are not that dumb and as far as I know you are alive. John, you are alive, aren't you, sweetheart? Khe Sanh is all over the news. I can't watch TV or read the paper without seeing something about marines trapped at Khe Sanh.

Damn it, O'Bryan, you better be alive! Write me right now. I love you! Be very, very careful.

Love, Susan

O'Bryan laughed and laid back on the flak jacket. He held Susan's letter in his right hand on his chest. He closed his eyes and with a smile on his face he dozed next to the trench. He drifted off into a light semi-sleep. The next thing he heard was the crack of a rifle round as it went overhead. He awakened from sleep in mid-air, rolling off the edge into the trench. As he hit the bottom, he knew Casey was dead.

Marines were already yelling "Corpsman!" as O'Bryan leaped from the trench, rolled then ran and dove the last five yards to Casey's side. Casey's silly glasses lay diagonally across his face. He lay on his back, and blood soaked his shirt from a single hole in the middle of his chest. Air bubbles and dark red blood spewed from the wound.

A corpsman arrived and bent quickly over Casey, then looked at O'Bryan and shook his head. "Right through the heart," the corpsman said and shook his head from side to side. "Help me get him in the trench."

The pages of the *Time* magazine fluttered in the wind next to Casey's clothed hand. O'Bryan looked at his friend's face. A grimace, or was it a smile, half formed there. He and the corpsman dragged Casey's body to the trench. A body bag and stretcher were fetched from grave's registration. O'Bryan and a mildly complaining marine carried the body along the dangerous above-ground route to the tin grave's registration shed next to the air strip.

It was dark when he returned to his bunker. He lit a candle and looked at his jungle shirt soaked with his friend's blood. He knew it was a mistake to allow someone too close again. He had vowed not to let it happen again but it had.

That night, he had the dream. The disembodied leg blasted in the air on an ambush long ago turning slowly in his mind. He awakened to the smell of his friend's blood, screaming to himself and the rats in the bunker.

The next few days O'Bryan said little. He studied the North Vietnamese assault trenches 500 meters away. The weather cleared, and F-4 Phantom jets made bombing run after bombing run on the N.V.A. trench line.

The marines watched and cheered at the napalm bursts. The Phantoms came in low, first dropping 250-

pound explosive bombs, the big silver cigar-shaped canisters of napalm directly on the N.V.A. trenches.

To the marines' amazement, after the napalm flash subsided, a few N.V.A. soldiers in the trench line fired several rifle volleys at the departing jet. That they survived the blast inspired awe, and that they had the guts to fire back commanded admiration even from O'Bryan's squad. It only served to fuel his quiet rage.

O'Bryan knew from other abandoned digs how they survived. They dug holes in the side of the trench near the bottom. Each hole was only large enough for one man to squeeze into. The hole went about four or five feet back, then down about five or six feet at a forty-five-degree angle. Only a direct or near direct hit of the hole would kill them. O'Bryan had noticed one flaw in this defense through his binoculars.

When the Phantom jet made its last pass and dropped napalm, all the oxygen was sucked form the trench and burned in the huge fireball.

With the aid of binoculars, he had seen their heads bob at the top of the trench line, gasping for air after clawing to the surface in the wake of the napalm blast. He smiled slowly as the idea took shape in his mind.

He found the Marine pilot assigned as forward air controller for the battalion and explained his idea. If the timing was right, it would be a fiery furnace for the N.V.A., with no escape.

The next day, the weather was clear. O'Bryan called in fire missions and registered all eight of the battalion's 81mm mortars on the area of the enemy trench where the napalm would be directed. As soon as the Phantom was well into his dive, O'Bryan called for twenty rounds of high-arching explosives from each gun.

He laid on top of his bunker with his binoculars for a good view of the inferno. It worked better than he had hoped for. The fireball washed over the trench, and tiny bobbing helmets appeared in the haze. The 160-round mortar barrage caught them all exposed as they came up for air.

O'Bryan could see body parts and equipment tossed in the air over the trench. Even faint screams could be heard. He laughed a sort of hysterical giggle at the sight. The tactic was very efficient.

Renarie approached O'Bryan as he slid down from the bunker. "That was some show, O'Bryan. Must have killed a hundred of the little fuckers. You know, if you was an officer, they would probably give you some kind of medal for that idea."

O'Bryan did not reply. He turned and went inside the dark dampness of his bunker. Renarie turned to Mike and pointed to O'Bryan's bunker. "See why he'll never be an officer? He don't have any social graces."

In two weeks' time, it was obvious to O'Bryan and everyone else at Khe Sahn that the siege was over. The sniper and rocket fire had ceased to be routine, and it was rumored that the First Air Cavalry was on its way up Route 9 with enough Huey Cobra gunships to blot out the sun. O'Bryan had even seen men sleeping on top of their bunkers. He sat atop his bunker, knees drawn to his chest in the chill evening as night shadows moved across the hillsides. *They are broken,* he thought. *There will be no American Dien Bien Phu.*

"O'Bryan!"

He knew it was Gunny Timmons before he twisted

around and saw the food-caked mustache.

"Here, Gunny," he replied.

"The lieutenant sent me to see if you want to go with some A.R.V.N. Rangers tomorrow. They're goin' out to see what's left in those N.V.A. trenches. They want someone with them, can call in mortar fire. Mr. Henderson figured you might like to see how effective your fire missions have been on 'em."

"How many you figure there's left out there, Gunny?"

"Looks like most of them that could, hauled ass for the Loation Border. Probably just left a few behind to slow us up."

"I'll need a radio operator. This is a volunteer thing, right, Gunny?"

"Strictly volunteer."

"OK, I volunteer Renarie."

"I'll tell him he volunteered. He'll be proud."

"What time we jump off, Gunny?"

"Be over at the South Vietnamese Ranger C.P. at 0700 hours. They got some kind of Army Captain advisor can fill you in on what they want you to do."

CHAPTER TWENTY

Nguyen was carried by two men down the assault trench and placed sitting up in the trench bottom. There were thirty other wounded who could not walk and would never survive the trip across to the Laotion border. A political officer he had never seen before knelt in the middle of the group and began to speak.

"Comrades, you have fought bravely and well. Because of your wounds, you will not be able to move from there with us. Your sacrifice will allow many others to live and fight another time, another place. Your names will be learned by school children as long as our country survives. We are leaving you some food, water, and plenty of ammunition. Fight on as long as you can. Kill as many Americans as you can. I salute you."

With that, each wounded man was given a weapon, ammunition, a little rice, and some dried fish. The men sat five to ten meters apart. In the space between them lay dead North Vietnamese comrades.

Nguyen looked around at the dying and dead. The finality of it all sank in at once. He knew none of them would leave this trench alive and he was part of this. His death was merely a formality. *This is how and where I will end,* he thought.

He allowed himself the luxury of a hashish-laced cigarette given to him by one of the medics. There were no other pain killers. The shrapnel and burns to his legs hurt. Several tourniquets had been used to stop the bleeding. He looked at the shattered, burned legs. He knew they would never work again, but it didn't matter now.

He felt more alone that he had ever felt in his life. The political officer was a liar, and he, along with the other wounded, knew it very well. No one in his country would remember his name, and only a few would mourn his loss. There were too many names to remember, too many losses to mourn. *She will remember me,* he thought. Thinking of her, he smiled.

His blood-caked hand fumbled with the button on his shirt pocket and removed the picture of them taken in Hanoi. He leaned sideways and lay on his back. It was difficult to see her face in the shadows of the trench. Then darkness overcame him.

At 0800 hours, O'Bryan and Renarie followed the point A.R.V.N. Platoon of the Black Panther Ranger Battalion out of their trenches toward the North Vietnamese trench line. Renarie swore as they began the assault, "I'll never fuckin' forgive you if I get killed doin' this worthless shit!"

"Think of it this way," O'Bryan said over his shoulder. "Someday, when your kid asks you, 'Dad, where were you when the shit hit the fan?' you can say, 'Standing right next to the fan, Son.'"

"That's just great," Renarie replied, "except, if I get my balls blown off, then there won't be no kid!"

The Rangers formed a long skirmish line to their front and made a great show of shooting from the hip and yelling as they ran toward the nearly lifeless trench line. O'Bryan could hear Renarie breathing hard behind him as he paused to get his bearings on his map.

"Tell me this, O'Bryan. If these little Ranger assholes are as bad as they pretend to be, how come they need us to go along with 'em?"

"Relax and enjoy the show, Renarie. This is all for the press, our noble South Vietnam allies takin' back their country."

An AK-47 opened up full automatic to their front. Bullets slapped into several men to O'Bryan's front, and the whole Battalion assault stopped in its tracks.

O'Bryan fumbled with an M33 hand grenade, pulled the pin, and tossed it into the N.V.A. trench twenty meters ahead. The grenade exploded, and there was no more fire from the trench. The Rangers rose to their feet, and O'Bryan followed as they swept into the trench.

The smell of over a thousand charred bodies greeted them as they dropped into the trench. It overcame Renarie immediately and he began to vomit. O'Bryan saw South Vietnamese Rangers firing blindly into dead and dying North Vietnamese who littered the bottom of the trench. He walked away from the firing around a corner of the winding assault trench and spotted movement next to several blackened bodies.

He raised his rifle and pointed it at the half burned face of a North Vietnamese soldier. He had started to squeeze the trigger but hesitated. The burned face was smiling. Advancing closer with his rifle still at his shoulder, O'Bryan saw the man was looking at a photo. He carefully studied the ragged, wounded man but could see no weapons or wires of any sort near him. O'Bryan lowered the M16.

He knelt next to the man and could see that the soldier held a color photo of himself in his khaki uniform alongside a young woman with long black hair, also in a khaki uniform.

The North Vietnamese looked at him with glazed eyes. A faint smile faded slowly from his face. The man raised the photo a few inches from his chest. O'Bryan inched closer to the man and took the picture. He studied it for a moment then carefully placed it into the soldier's blood-spattered shirt pocket.

O'Bryan stood and slung his rifle upside down. He bent and lifted the North Vietnamese over his shoulder.

Nguyen grunted in pain. His blood streamed down the front of O'Bryan's flak jacket.

O'Bryan stepped out of the trench and began walking back to the Khe Sanh perimeter.

"Where you goin' with the dead gook?" yelled Renarie after him. O'Bryan did not answer. He did not look back.

O'Bryan knew as he walked that he had more in common with the man he carried than any of the civilian people in his own country who had sent him here. He also knew that neither he nor the man he carried would ever be the same again. The war was over for both of them. No matter what else happened, they had won.

On a mountainside three miles Northwest in Laos, a tiger crouched in the darkness of the triple canopy jungle floor. He sat motionless watching a line of half-clad North Vietnamese porters.

The men wore traditional black straw conical hats and baggy black pants rolled to their knees. Their feet were clad in sandals made from old tire treads and pieces of rubber inner tubing. They carried poles with bundles attached at each end and balanced across one shoulder. Some pushed bicycles laden with over 200 pounds of food, ammunition, or medical supplies. In the canopy-covered network of trails, the men felt safe from American bombs.

One man laid his bicycle with its bulging packs slowly on its side next to the trail. He walked twenty feet up the hillside unknowingly towards the tiger. He loosened his rope belt and lowered his pants. He looked around once then squatted to relieve himself.

The tiger raised slightly. He had been driven to this area by the constant bombing and shelling around Khe Sanh. This was his new territory. He had lost his mate to the bombs and now hunted alone.

He looked at the squatting man intently with burning eyes as massive muscles tensed for the strike. He had learned to hate and kill men at Khe Sanh.

About Atmosphere Press

Atmosphere Press is an independent, full-service publisher for excellent books in all genres and for all audiences. Learn more about what we do at atmospherepress.com.

We encourage you to check out some of Atmosphere's latest releases, which are available at Amazon.com and via order from your local bookstore:

Rags to Rags, nonfiction by Ellie Guzman
On a Lark, a novel by Sandra Fox Murphy
Ivory Tower, a novel by Grant Matthew Jenkins
Tailgater, short stories by Graham Guest
Plastic Jesus and Other Stories, short stories by Judith Ets-Hokin
The Quintessents, a novel by Clem Fiorentino
The Devil's in the Details, short stories by VA Christie
Heat in the Vegas Night, nonfiction by Jerry Reedy
Chimera in New Orleans, a novel by Lauren Savoie
The Neurosis of George Fairbanks, a novel by Jonathan Kumar
Blue Screen, a novel by Jim van de Erve
Evelio's Garden, nonfiction by Sandra Shaw Homer
Difficulty Swallowing, essays by Kym Cunningham
Come Kill Me!, short stories by Mackinley Greenlaw
The Unexpected Aneurysm of the Potato Blossom Queen, short stories by Garrett Socol
Gathered, a novel by Kurt Hansen
Unorthodoxy, a novel by Joshua A.H. Harris

About the Author

Charles McIntyre is a Marine Vietnam veteran who spent twenty-six months in Vietnam from August 1966 thru October of 1968. He served the entire time with the First Battalion of the Twenty-Sixth Marine Regiment. He participated in twenty-one ground combat operations including the siege of Khe Sanh.

He left active duty in 1969 and attended the University of Oklahoma and the University of Central Oklahoma, obtaining a B.S. in Liberal Arts Studies. He is retired from the Oklahoma City Police Department where he spent thirty years. He and his wife Jan reside in Oklahoma City, Oklahoma.

CPSIA information can be obtained
at www.ICGtesting.com
Printed in the USA
LVHW031733190220
647495LV00006B/1050